in Germany,
Austria, and Switzerland

The all-in-one travel and language guide

Uli Bonk and Robert Tilley

PASSPORT BOOKS
NTC/Contemporary Publishing Company

Library of Congress Cataloging-in-Publication Data
is available from the United States Library of Congress

Photographs
All photographs by Narinda Peter Albaum, except the following:

Cover photo: Zefa Pictures
Pictor International—London p1, 2, 3, 4, 9(b), 14(t), 15, 17(t), 18(b),
20, 26, 27(b), 28, 30(t), 35(t), back cover (t)
The Image Bank p5, 9(t), 10, 11, 13
Robert Harding Picture Library p14(b), 16, 17(b), 18(t), 19, 21, 22, 23,
24, 25, 30(b)
Getty Images p27(t), 29, 31, 33, 35(b), back cover (m, b)
Life File p32, 60(t)
Cephas p61(l), 71(t), 73(t), 76, 81(r), 82, 84, 85(t, b), 86, 87(b)
Anthony Blake p70(t), 71(b), 75, 79(t), 80, 83, 85(m), 87(b), spine

This edition published by Passport Books
An imprint of NTC/Contemporary Publishing Company
4255 West Touhy Avenue
Lincolnwood (Chicago), Illinois 60646-1975 U.S.A.

Published in cooperation with BBC Worldwide Ltd. "BBC" and the
BBC logotype are trademarks of the British Broadcasting Corporation
and are used under license.
© BBC Worldwide Ltd 1998.
Printed in the United Kingdom

International Standard Book Number: 0-8442-0152-9 book
International Standard Book Number: 0-8442-0163-4 package
1   3   5   7   9   11   12   10   8   6   4   2

INTRODUCTION

Get Around in Germany, Austria, and Switzerland will enable you to
pick up the language, travel with confidence and experience the
very best the country has to offer. You can use it both *before* a trip,
to pick up the basics of the language and to plan your itinerary,
and *during* your trip, as a phrasebook and as a source of practical
information in all the key travel situations.

Contents
Insider's guide to Germany An introduction to the country,
a guide to the main cities and region-by-region highlights for
planning itineraries
Bare necessities The absolute essentials of German
Seven main chapters Covering key travel situations from *Getting*
around to *Entertainment and leisure*. Each chapter has three main
sections: *information* to help you understand the local way of
doing things; *Phrasemaker*, a phrasebook of key words and
phrases; *Language works/Try it out*, simple dialogues and activities
to help you remember the language.
Menu reader A key to menus in German
Language builder A simple introduction to German grammar
1000-word dictionary The most important German words you
will come across with their English translations.
Sounds German A clear guide to pronouncing the language

How to use the book
Before you go You can use the *Insider's guide* to get a flavor
of the country and plan where you want to go. To pick up the
language, the *Phrasemaker* sections give you the key words and
phrases; the *Language works* dialogues show the language in action,
and *Try it out* offers you a chance to practice for yourself.

During your trip The *Insider's guide* offers tips on the best things
to see and do in the main cities. The *Phrasemaker* works as a
phrasebook with all the key language to help you get what you
want. Within each chapter there is also practical "survival"
information to help you get around and understand the country.

Insider's guide to Germany

Despite its outward appearance of stability, Germany has had a more turbulent recent history than most countries, and the

rock-like image it presents to the outside world could be misleading. Modern Germany took its shape from an untidy jumble of autonomous states little more than a century ago, and since then the country has suffered two devastating world wars, one of which was provoked by the worst dictatorship Europe has ever seen and which left the defeated country divided into two opposing ideological halves. Reunited by the collapse of Communism, Germany is still trying to rediscover its original social and political integration, at a cost which is paradoxically causing even greater disunity. It's by no means a happy country: uncertain about its role within Europe, unhappy about its image abroad, unsettled by predictions of social unrest and political upheaval. Today Bismarck, founding father of the present German state, would undoubtedly be a member of the growing ranks of pessimists. For all the uncertainty – perhaps because of it – Germany remains a very vital, even vibrant country. The cultural tradition rooted in the music of Bach, Beethoven and Wagner and in the works of Goethe and Schiller lives on, through the talents of outstanding younger generations of composers, musicians and writers. Theaters are full and the film industry is entering a boom following the recovery of the Babelsberg studios. Popular music is shedding its sentimental, "folksy"

Rhinish Castle

Heidelberg

garb and competing with the best from the United States and Britain, architects are busy recreating the war-destroyed or run-down historic centers of east Berlin, Dresden and Leipzig, while pampered west German cities such as Cologne, Hamburg and Munich are rising energetically to the new challenges from a highly competitive east. The regional policies of the European Union help Germany's 15 federal states establish and maintain their strong historical traditions, with the Protestant North forming a religious community of interests balanced by the Catholic weight of the South. This web of mutual and opposing characteristics gives Germany a tough fabric which might yet confound the pessimists and keep the country a central force for stability within Europe. It certainly makes it the multi-faceted country face which so fascinates tourists – from the beaches of the North Sea and Baltic coasts to the fir-clad slopes and craggy peaks of the Bavarian and Allgäu Alps, a 600-mile (1,000 kilometers) journey from the flat heathland north of Hamburg to the foothills of the Alps. Scarcely anywhere else in Europe (not even France) is there such a broad range of clearly-defined regional differences, from folk customs to food and drink. In the latter area alone, Germans display their differences like a badge, with the Bavarians making a ritual of drinking beer while Rhinelanders cultivate respect for their fine white wines.

Germany's diversity extends to its climate, making the country a year-round tourist destination. Its cold winters guarantee ski enthusiasts good snow conditions in Alpine resorts from November until the late spring, while the lower heights of the Black Forest and central German upland stretches such as the Eifel and Harz are usually covered with snow for at least two months of the year. Warm summers mean high season for the seaside resorts of the North Sea and Baltic coasts, where broad stretches of sands and rolling dunes offer escape from the crowds which pack Mediterranean beaches at this time of year. Spring sometimes comes late, but it takes only a few hours of March or April sunshine to bring café tables on to the pavements of Berlin and Hamburg and to persuade Bavarian beer gardens to open up. In Bavaria the beer garden season extends until the first frosts of November chill the liter mugs of ale. Fall is a truly golden time of year. In southern Germany, September and October are invariably warm and mellow, with skies of a penetrating blue which the Bavarians have incorporated into their state flag. This is the time, too, to visit the country's warmest corner, the southwest slopes of the Black Forest and the nearby Bodensee (Lake Constance), where citrus trees and palms flourish in the balmy air. But even when Germany is shrouded in November mists or in February gloom, a packed cultural calendar offers a wealth of diversions. In all the large cities there's at least one cultural festival per month. Regional and city tourist offices have details and issue monthly brochures in English, listing events and explaining how to book tickets.

Travel with only the amount of cash you need for everyday needs, using credit cards, traveler's checks or Eurochecks issued by European banks for larger purchases and hotel bills. Eurochecks are a particularly favorable form of payment, because your home bank calculates an exchange rate considerably better than that for cross-counter currency transactions. The checks take at least two weeks to clear, giving you a form of interest-free credit. Cash machines, allowing you to withdraw cash using your bank or credit card, are to be found in all but the smallest towns, and in cities they are practically on every street corner. It's advisable to check with your bank about the most favorable form of collecting cash and changing money within Germany; rates vary greatly from bank to bank. All the major

credit cards are accepted by most hotels, the German airline Lufthansa and the country's railway authority (Deutsche Bahn) and virtually all the larger shops and department stores. In some smaller shops and boutiques you might be offered a discount if you pay in cash instead of with a credit card, but otherwise bargaining is taboo.

Bonn Embassies
USA: Deichmanns Aue, 0228/3391
Canada: Godesberger Allee 119,
tel. 0228/810060
UK: Friedrich Ebert Allee 77,
tel. 0228/234061
Ireland: Godesberger Allee 119,
tel. 0228/376937

South Africa: Auf der Hostert 3,
tel. 0228/82010
Australia: Godesberger Allee 105-
107, tel. 0228/81030
New Zealand: Bonn-Center,
tel. 0228/228070

Bamberg

Holidays, festivals and events

Film festivals Saarbrücken
(January), Berlin (February),
Munich (June).

Music festivals Munich ballet
festival (April); Dresden Musikfest-
spiele, Hamburg ballet festival
(May); Händel Festival, Halle,
"Music Days," Leipzig, Mozart
Festival, Würzburg (June); Bach
Festival, Berlin, Munich opera

festival (July); Bad Hersfeld opera
festival, European Music Festival,
Stuttgart, Richard Wagner Festival,
Bayreuth (August); Berlin "Festival
Weeks" (September); International
Beethoven festival, Bonn
(September–October).

Theater "Theater der Welt" festival,
Essen (July), Heidelberg Castle
Festival (August).

Sports Grand Slam tennis tournament, Munich, International ski-jumping championships, Garmisch-Partenkirchen (January); German Open tennis tournament, Hamburg (May); Kiel regatta week (June); Mercedes Cup tennis tournament, Stuttgart (July); BMW international golf tournament, Eschenried, near Munich, Baden-Baden racing week (August); Six-day cycle race, Munich (December).

Folk festivals, beer and wine festivals Carnival (Fasching in southern Germany), throughout the winter but climaxing in February and ending in a wild splurge on Shrove Tuesday (Shrove Monday, Rosenmontag, processions in Mainz, Cologne and other Rhineland towns); Starkbier (strong beer) festival, Munich (February); summer open-air theater and music festivals in most cities and major towns (particularly attractive programs in Berlin, Hamburg, Frankfurt, Wiesbaden and Munich); "Rhine in Flames" fireworks festival along the banks of the Rhine (August), wine festivals in the vineyard towns of the Rhine, Mosel, Main, Neckar, Saar, Ruwer, Elbe (around Meißen), the Rhineland-Palatinate "Wine Road" villages and on the wine-producing slopes of the Black Forest (August– October); Germany's biggest wine festival is the Dürkheimer Wurstmarkt (mid-September); Kulmbach beer festival, held in the northern Bavarian town which produces the world's strongest beer (late July to early August); Oktoberfest, the famous Munich beer festival (late September to mid-October); Christmas markets (Weihnachtsmärkte) from early December until December 24 in cities, towns and most villages throughout the country (Nuremberg's is the most spectacular).

Munich beer hall

Berlin

*G*ermany's huge capital city is a sprawling metropolis, covering a larger area than any other in Europe. Divided into two halves for nearly 30 years by the infamous Berlin Wall, it still displays enormous contrasts and there's almost a palpable demarcation line still between East and West. Three decades of Communism will continue to show their mark for many years. Yet some central streets – notably Friedrichstraße – are rapidly recovering the style they had when Berlin competed with Paris for the 1920s' title of European capital of fun.

Brandenburg Gate

Don't miss

A ride through central Berlin from the Tiergarten to the Brandenburger Tor on the top deck of a number 100 Berlin bus.
A visit to the Berlin Wall museum at Checkpoint Charlie, the most famous crossing point between the two Berlins during the Cold War.
A stroll down Unter den Linden, the tree-lined avenue which was once a center of Berlin cosmopolitan society.

A wander through the Fischerinsel area, the medieval heart of Berlin with much of its historic character still intact.
An after-dark walk down the Kurfürstendamm – the city's famous Ku'damm – where more than 100 taverns, clubs, restaurants and cafés pulsate with life.
A morning or afternoon in the Pergamon Museum, named after the monumental Greek temple shipped to Berlin piece by piece in the 19th century and rebuilt beneath the vast roof of its new home.

A lift ride up the Fernsehturm on Alexanderplatz for the best view of Berlin. Berliners are proud to tell you that their Fernsehturm is higher than the Eiffel Tower.

A stroll around the palace and grounds of Schloß Charlottenburg, the residence of Prussian rulers from 1695 until the end of the monarchy.

A visit to the longest remaining section of the Berlin Wall, between Mühlenstraße and the Oberbaumbrücke, a 0.8-mile stretch of concrete decorated with frescos by more than 100 international painters.

A walk or a cycle ride through the Grunewald woods, the lovely swath of countryside which is the Berliners' playground in all winds and weathers.

A shopping trip to the KaDeWe department store, one of the biggest in continental Europe with a delicatessen section of enormous scale and scope.

Clubs and bars

Café Westfal, on east Berlin's Kollwitzplatz, was a center of anti-regime, reformist activism during the Communist era and is still very much part of the fringe scene.

Siegessäule

Chez Nous (Marburgerstraße 14), Germany's most outrageous drag-show club with two nightly performances reminiscent of Isherwood's Berlin of the 1920s.

Ku'dorf (Joachimsthaler-straße 15, just off the Ku'damm) is an underground warren of 18 Kneipen (or bars) serving beers from every Berlin brewery and many more.

Metropol, on Nollendorfplatz, has two dance floors and regular theme evenings, ranging from laser shows to gay get-togethers.

Quasimodo (Kantstraße 12a) offers some of Berlin's best jazz in a smokey basement atmosphere.

Wilhelm Hoeck, in the Wilmersdorf district, is Berlin's oldest Kneipe, with a fine Jugendstil interior and a cross-section of Berlin as clientele.

Fernsehturm

Have a coffee or a pastry in

Café Adler, which used to nestle up to the Berlin Wall at Checkpoint Charlie and which is redolent not only of the aromatic coffee it serves but with the memories of the Cold War past.

Café Mosaik, between Alexanderplatz and the Rotes Rathaus, where the French influence on the Prussian court of centuries past is still evident in the choice of wines and bistro dishes.

Café Einstein, a short walk from the KaDeWe department store, where the name alone gives you an idea of the kind of intellectual crowd who make this atmospheric Berlin hang-out their regular haunt.

Have a meal in

Blockhaus Nikolskoe, tucked away in a romantic, lakeside location in the Glienecker Park and originally built by Prussian King Wilhelm III for his daughter Charlotte, who married Russian Tsar Nicholas I.

Hardtke, on central Meinekestraße, a simple, wood-paneled, tavern-style restaurant with a basic but excellent menu to match.

Turmstuben, which is literally wrapped around the inside of the cupola of the Französischer Dom (the French Cathedral) on east Berlin's lovely Gendarmenmarkt, recommended, however, only for those with a head for heights and the stamina to climb the winding staircase to get there.

Zitadellen-Schänke, a historic vaulted restaurant within the sturdy walls of Spandau's castle, the Zitadelle, which serves a banquet-style menu to match the surroundings.

Zur Letzten Instanz, which takes its name ("the final appeal") from the nearby law courts in east Berlin and which was frequented during its long and colorful history by such diverse guests as Napoleon and Gorbachev.

Children's Berlin

Berlin's zoo – the Zoologischer Garten – is Germany's largest, with more than 14,000 animals. Its birdhouse is the largest in Europe and houses many rare species. Children love the evil-looking crocodiles of the terrarium and the penguins and dolphins of the aquarium.

Transportation

City buses

Berlin's distinctive, cream-colored double-decker buses run on all central routes, and an extensive network covers all suburbs and outlying districts. All-night services are indicated by the letter N displayed on bus stops.

The subway

Berlin's subway system – the combined U-Bahn and S-Bahn – is the largest in continental Europe. Important stations for visitors include Zoologischer Garten (for the Ku'damm and central shopping districts), Friedrichstraße and Alexanderplatz (for east Berlin and the most important city museums).

Day trips from Berlin

Frankfurt an der Oder, an hour's drive or train ride east of Berlin, is not a particularly picturesque city but holds the fascination of having a Polish town as a direct neighbor, the two communities separated only by a bridge across the Oder river.

Potsdam is a must for any visitor to Berlin, a historic and finely restored town whose chief attraction is Frederick the Great's beautiful summer home, Sanssouci, but also the location of Schloß Cecilienhof, the country mansion (now a hotel) where American President Truman, British Prime Minister Atlee and Soviet leader Stalin drew up the 1945 Potsdam agreement.

Hamburg

*G*ermany's most important port is also the country's third favorite tourist destination and competes energetically with Munich for the number-two position. This North–South rivalry extends to hotly contested comparisons of the numbers of hours of sunshine enjoyed by each city and the extent of each other's rainfall. The comparisons are really unnecessary, as both cities are vastly different in appearance and character. Each has its special flair. Hamburg's is more subtle than Munich's. The city has to contend with its salty, slightly sleazy image, although first-time visitors are invariably pleasantly surprised by its elegance and urbane sophistication. The first stretch of water encountered is not the harbor but the two inland lakes – the Binnenalster and the Außenalster – around which Hamburg's most expensive residential areas and shopping districts are grouped. Two of Germany's finest hotels overlook the Binnenalster, which is lined on one side by a graceful avenue of Jugendstil homes described as "millionaires' row." Hamburg's own Jugendstil style provides another notable contrast to the Munich city panorama, where buildings of this period have a far more ponderous look. The harbor sector, of course, is quite unique, with docklands as well preserved as London's. An unofficial kind of preservation order has also been placed on the "naughty" bits of Hamburg, harbor backstreets and the famous Reeperbahn, where some of Europe's most explicit sex shows and cabarets are tolerated with a typical Hamburg "laissez-faire" shrug.

Don't miss

A boat trip around the huge harbor, with its endless quays and dry docks.
A nighttime tour of the Reeperbahn area, home of Europe's most famous "red light" districts.
A cycle ride around Hamburg's two inland lakes, the Binnenalster and the Außenalster.
The Sunday morning Fischmarkt at the St. Pauli jetties, more like a weekly festival than an ordinary fish market.

A rowboat excursion through the canals and backwaters of the Stadtpark, the city's largest park.
A visit to the Oevelgönne harbor museum to see its fascinating collection of restored old ships.

Clubs and bars

Cotton Club, Hamburg's oldest and best-known jazz club, on central Alter Steinweg.
Große Freiheit 36, lively but respectable dance club and disco which shares the same St. Pauli street (Große Freiheit) with several of the area's hottest sex-spots.

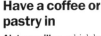

Have a coffee or pastry in

Alsterpavillon, which looks out over the Binnenalster from its vantage point on the Jungfernstieg.
Destille, on the first floor of the arts and crafts museum, the Museum für Kunst und Gewerbe.

Have a meal in

Fischereihafen Restaurant, in the Altona district, where freshly-caught fish are the basis of the daily-changing menu.
Fischerhaus, part of the fish market (Fischmarkt) and the place to eat eel soup and other Hamburg specialities.
Landhaus Dill, a stylish restaurant in a fine turn-of-the-century mansion overlooking the Elbe estuary.

Munich

*M*unich's long-held reputation as the "secret capital of Germany" has been lost with the reunification of Berlin and the ambitious reconstruction programs in such rival cities as Dresden and Leipzig. Yet Munich (or München, to give the city its German name) still manages to attract more visitors than any other city with the exception of Berlin. They are drawn by its now legendary lifestyle, an elusive combination of chic urbanity and rough-spun Bavarian charm. It's a city of beer halls and sleek restaurants, brass bands and exquisite chamber music ensembles, Mediterranean-style markets and glittering boutiques – the contrasts are virtually endless and sometimes bewildering. Its social and cultural calendar is so packed with events that it gives the impression of being caught up in an unending party, climaxing with the famous Oktoberfest beer festival. Beer seems to rule the city, and even the annual wine festival is held in a beer hall. On warm days in spring, summer and fall the beer gardens beckon enticingly, while in winter the taverns of the Altstadt (old town), Haidhausen and Schwabing – the old artists' quarter – offer cozy retreats for enjoying a glass of ale and a dish of Bavarian specialties (usually some form of sausage or roast pork).

Don't miss

A ride on streetcar number 19,
which takes in most of the major city-
center sights on its journey from the
main rail station, the Hauptbahnhof,
to Haidhausen.

A simple Bavarian lunch at one of
the beer-and-snack stands in the
main market, the Viktualienmarkt.

**High mass at one of the many city-
center churches** (preferably the
cathedral, the Dom); check out in the
daily newspaper *Süddeutsche Zeitung*
where and when a full choral mass is
being sung.

**A bike ride through the Englischer
Garten park,** from south to north
(there's a bike-rental business at the
Veterinärstraße entrance to the
park).

A swim in the elaborately decorated,
marble-pillared and tiled Jugendstil
surroundings of the Müllersches
Volksbad pool, Rosenheimerstraße.

**A visit to the Lenbachhaus art
gallery,** a Tuscany-style city
mansion and home to some of the
finest works by Kandinsky, Klee and
other members of the Blauer Reiter
group of artists.

**A tour of the immense Deutsches
Museum.**

**A visit to the opera at Munich's
Staatstheater,** followed by a late
stroll along fashionable Maximilianstraße, with its smart shops and bars.

A liter mug of beer at one of the
heavy oak tables of the Hofbräuhaus,
Munich's beer "temple."

**A wander around the Schwabing
district,** where commemorative
plaques on many of the fine
Jugendstil mansions recall such
famous former residents as
Lenin and Paul Klee.

Clubs and bars

The Hotel Vierjahreszeiten bar,
where an elderly pianist tinkers away
until 9 pm, when the scene shifts to
the nearby, handkerchief-sized
dance floor.

Schumann's bar, on fashionable
Maximilianstraße. Owner Charles
Schumann oversees a team of
talented barmen, who shake and mix
Munich's largest range of cocktails.

Käfer's Odeonsplatz bistro and bar,
where the chic crowd gather around
a large concert grand piano and
exchange pleasantries and telephone
numbers.

The Schwabinger Podium, one of
Munich's oldest jazz haunts, on a
small back street in the heart of the
city's former artists' quarter.

Viktualienmarkt

Have a meal in

Augustiner Gaststätte, a beautifully
decorated Jugendstil restaurant on
the pedestrian shopping precinct,
serving deliciously nutty beer from
Munich's oldest brewery.

Dürnbräu, a side street off central
Tal, where you'll share one of the
long trestle tables with regulars who
drink their beer from personal,
pewter-capped mugs or – in fine
weather – find a corner in one of the
two delightful terrace-gardens.

**Hundskugel, a short walk from
Marienplatz,** Munich's oldest
tavern (dating back to the mid-
15th century), with a centuries-old
tradition of best Bavarian cooking.

Pfälzer Weinprobierstube, once part of the Wittelsbach royal palace but now a vast, vaulted and echoing series of rooms where you're expected to drink one of the wide range of Palatinate (Pfälzer) wines that share the menu with a limited variety of German specialty dishes.

Day trips from Munich

Starnberg lake – the Starnberger See – a half-hour car drive south or a journey of similar length on the metropolitan railway, the S-Bahn. The lake has several quiet resorts and a memorial site marking the place where King Ludwig II was found drowned.

Children's Munich

Munich's zoo, in the Thalkirchen district, is one of Germany's best, with few cages and maximum freedom for its animals. Further south, in the leafy Grünewald suburb, is one of the country's leading movie studios, Bavaria Studios, where stunt shows are a popular feature of the daily tours for the public.

Transportation

Munich has a highly efficient network of buses, streetcars and subways (the U-Bahn). Tickets (including a very reasonably priced day pass) cover travel on all three. Useful junctions include: **Karlsplatz** (also known as Stachus) and **Marienplatz,** for the central city. **Münchner Freiheit,** for Schwabing and the Olympic grounds.

Dachau, a pretty hilltop town and artists' colony, with a moving memorial to the infamous concentration camp.

Oktoberfest

13

Northern Germany

*A*lthough it's not geographic-
ally clear where northern
Germany begins (north of the
*Main River or on the plains of Lower
Saxony, north of the Teutoburger
Forest?), the region certainly has a
clearly defined end: the Schleswig
Holstein border with Denmark.
Schleswig Holstein, a wind-swept peninsula of dykes, polders, moors
and low-built thatch-roofed farms, is also a natural division between
Germany's two seaside areas: the North Sea beaches and dunes and
the even wilder sands of the Baltic. Two of Germany's official
vacation routes, the Grüne Küstenstraße and the Nordsee- and Ostsee-
Bäderstraße, follow the coastal stretch from the Dutch border in the
west to the Danish frontier in the north and the Polish border in the east,
taking in Bremen, Hamburg and Lübeck on the way.*

Don't miss

An excursion to one of the Ostfriesische (East Frisian) islands, little more than large sandbanks strung out like a necklace a few kilometers from the North Sea coast.

A detour to the bleak Ahlhorn Heide (heath), south of Oldenburg, to view Germany's own Stonehenge, the Visbecker Bräutigam (Visbeck Bridegroom), a huge pile of granite blocks built by Stone Age people for a purpose as mysterious as the heath itself.

A train ride to the most popular and fashionable of the Nordfriesische (North Frisian) islands, Sylt, linked to the mainland by a causeway.

A walk over the mudflats (the Watten) to one of the Nordfriesische "Halligen," the smaller islands accessible by foot when the tide is out. Don't attempt the walk alone, however, but join one of the tours offered at most resorts (rubber boots are included in the price of the tour!).

A boat trip from Wilhelmshaven, Bremerhaven or Cuxhaven.

A day out in Lübeck, finest of the former Hanseatic League cities, distinguished by its striking red-brick architecture – and by its associations with the writer Thomas Mann, born here in 1875.

A night out in the casino at Travemünde, Germany's oldest seaside resort.

A train ride from the port of Rostock to one of the sleepy seaside resorts of the Mecklenburger Bucht, or to the picturesque old town of Stralsund and from there by bus across the causeway to the holiday island of Rügen, with its endless dunes and beaches.

A boat excursion (from Cuxhaven or Hamburg) to the island of Helgoland, an isolated outpost halfway between the North Frisian and East Frisian islands. Its strategic position at the approaches to the Elbe river and the port of Hamburg made Helgoland a hotly contested prize, which passed back and forth between Denmark, Britain and Germany. Virtually every building on the island was destroyed by the Allies in the final weeks of the Second World War. Today it's a popular tourist destination, with two fine beaches (one of them a nudist colony).

Travemünde

The Rhineland

*T*he river Rhine (German: Rhein) runs the length of Germany, from the Swiss border to the Netherlands, and then to the North Sea. The section known as the Rhineland, however, is the 80-mile stretch from Mainz to Koblenz, the spectacular river valley everyone knows from countless calendar and postcard pictures. Castles mark its route like milestones, perched on the hilly banks and in one case in the middle of the river itself. Germany's most select vineyards tumble down riverside slopes, embracing sleepy little towns and villages which shake themselves awake when wine festival time arrives.

Burg Katz

Don't miss

The castles of the Rhine

Burg Katz and Burg Maus, a pair of castles named "cat and mouse" because of the rivalry between their medieval owners.

Burg Rheinstein, near Bingen, last resting place of its most famous owner, Prince Friedrich von Preußen, who transformed it from a medieval ruin to a romantic castle.

Burg Reichenstein, near Bingen, now a luxurious hotel and restaurant.

Burg Rheinfels, perched on the same rocky outcrop as the famous Lorelei, the prow-shaped cliff named after a river siren who is blamed for luring boatsmen to their deaths in the swirling river current below.

Burg Sonneck, a favorite castle of Prussian King Friedrich Wilhelm IV.

Marksburg, the only one of the many Rhine castles to have survived centuries of strife and siege intact. It houses a fascinating collection of weapons and ancient manuscripts.
Mauseturm, not a castle at all, but a former customs post clinging to a tiny island near Bingen.
Schloß Brömserburg, Rüdesheim, with one of the region's most interesting wine museums.
Schloß Johannesberg, in the Rheingau, whose wines are extremely prestigious. This is also the source of one of Germany's finest Sekts (sparkling wines), the "von Metternich."

The Rhineland cities

Bonn Although it has lost its importance on the German political map, Bonn is still a major cultural center, the birthplace of Ludwig van Beethoven, commemorated by a museum in the house where he was born (Bonngasse 20).
Cologne The chief city of the Rhineland, worth a wide detour just to admire its amazing cathedral, or Dom, repository of a gold and silver reliquary believed to contain relics of the Magi, the three kings who paid homage to the infant Jesus. The Dom is an enormously impressive example of the Gothic style. Cologne has much else of interest, including

Cologne

one of Germany's finest art museum complexes, the Wallraf-Richarts-Museum and Museum Ludwig.
Koblenz This city, founded by the Romans, stands at the confluence of the Rhine and the river Mosel, whose meandering course as far as Trier is well worth following, either by road or better still on one of the excursion boats which bustle up and down between its vine-hung banks.
Mainz Site of the most northerly of the three great Romanesque cathedrals of the southern Rhine (the other two are at Speyer and Worms). One thousand years of German history can be traced within its dark interior. Visit Mainz on "Rosenmontag" or Shrove Tuesday and you'll be caught up in Germany's most extravagant carnival.

Eastern Germany

T his area of Germany has some of the country's major cultural cities and places of historical interest. At least three are well worth including on any tour itinerary.

Semper opera house

Dresden

Beautifully located on a sweeping bend of the Elbe river, Dresden was virtually obliterated in one British bombing raid in the closing stages of the Second World War. Reconstruction has been slow but the city is gradually regaining its old elegance.

Don't miss

The Albertinum, one of Germany's greatest art museums, converted from a royal arsenal by Saxony's King Albert as a suitable home for the art treasures he and his culturally minded forefathers had collected.

The Semper opera house Try and see an opera production in this graceful, Italian-style 19th-century opera house, named after the man who built it, Gottfried Semper. If you can't get tickets or there is no opera performance during your visit, you can still take part in a tour of its red-plush and gilt interior.

The Zwinger One of the world's greatest baroque ensembles, the Zwinger (actually meaning part of Dresden's original fortifications) is a beautifully decorative collection of buildings enclosing a central courtyard and garden, scene of extravagant parties during the 18th-century reign of its creator, August the Strong.

Weimar

The great poets Goethe and Schiller were neighbors in this beautifully restored old city, whose name is also forever engraved in German political history. Bach, Liszt and Carl Maria von Weber also called Weimar their home at various times.

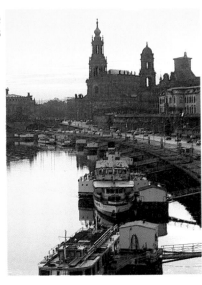

Don't miss

The Goethehaus, where the great poet spent 47 years of his life, and his Gartenhaus (Garden House), in parkland beside the river Ilm, where he enjoyed many happy hours. **The Historischer Friedhof** (Historic Cemetery), where Goethe and Schiller lie in neighboring tombs.

Leipzig

Eastern Germany's second largest city, a major trade fair center and a place of pilgrimage for music lovers, who pay homage at the grave of Johann Sebastian Bach. The grave is in the church where he was choirmaster for 27 years, the late-Gothic Thomaskirche. Other important stops on a Leipzig itinerary:
The Nikolaikirche, where thousands of East German reformers gathered every Monday in the months leading up to the collapse of Communism.
The Museum der Bildenden Künste, one of Germany's leading art galleries.

Stallhof Castle, Dresden

Southern Germany

*S*outhern Germany, the region south of the river Main, rises through a series of upland stretches of lovely countryside to the towering Alpine range which marks the border with Austria. In the West, the heavily wooded Black Forest (*Schwarzwald*) runs down to the river Rhine and the eastern border of France. In the East, the Allgäu Alps lead up to the higher and mightier Bavarian Alps. And in the southwest corner of Germany is the country's largest and most

beautiful lake, the Bodensee, its shores shared by Germany, Switzerland and Austria. This far corner of Germany enjoys the country's mildest climate, in which citrus trees thrive alongside palms and other flora. The Bodensee is Germany's apple orchard, while the west-facing slopes of the Black Forest produce some of the country's finest wines.

The Black Forest – dense woods and rolling hills

The Black Forest (Schwarzwald) is a year-round vacation destination, offering endless hiking routes and horseback riding trails in spring, summer and fall and challenging skiing in winter. While fashionable Baden-Baden has some of Germany's most luxurious and expensive hotels, there are innumerable farmhouses throughout the region where a featherbed and a hearty breakfast cost less than DM 50.

Baden-Baden Just DM 5 will buy you entrance to Germany's most exclusive casino, an investment that you might recoup with a bit of luck. Gentlemen should wear ties, and for the ladies this is the chance to unpack that little black dress. If luck is on your side, splurge with a meal or even an overnight stay at Brenner's Park Hotel, testing its claim to be one of the world's best.

Freiburg im Breisgau The Black Forest's chief town and worth visiting because of its magnificent cathedral, or Münster. It has a 16th-century triptych by Hans Baldung Grien and paintings by Holbein the Younger and Lucas Cranach the Elder.

Picturesque Black Forest towns and villages

Alpirsbach The 16th-century town hall has a fresco depicting the devil, blamed for burning the town down on many occasions. Sample the locally brewed beer; its fine flavor is attributed to the very pure properties of the local water.

Bad Herrenalb Railway buffs love the spa's 19th-century rail station, which originally belonged to nearby Baden-Baden. It was dismantled piece by piece when Baden-Baden built a new one and was re-erected in its new, picturesque site.

Bad Liebenzell The medicinal properties of the hot springs of this pretty spa were discovered back in the 15th century, although the Victorians really put the town on the map.

Calw Childhood home of the revered German writer Hermann Hesse, this pretty little market town – all half-timbered houses and steep gables – hasn't changed much since his birth there.

Freudenstadt The town's name means "City of Joy," thought to have been given to it by the refugees from religious persecution who found refuge there in the 17th century. It was one of Germany's most carefully planned Renaissance towns, with streets laid out in checkerboard fashion.

Triberg One of the main stops of the "Cuckoo Clock" tourist route. You can view many historic examples in the town's excellent natural history museum, the Schwarzwaldmuseum. Just outside the town are Germany's highest waterfalls, a 500ft plunge by the river Gutach.

Weil der Stadt You would never guess it, but this dreamy little town was once an important city of the Holy Roman Empire. Some well-preserved defense walls and fortifications are the only remaining evidence of its former importance.

Wölfach Glass is blown here just as it has been for centuries past. Ask at the Dorotheenhütte glassworks for a guided tour.

The Black Forest lakes

The region has some very beautiful lakes:

Mummelsee, a small lake in a forest clearing that local lore says harbors sprites and other woodland creatures of fantasy.

Schluchsee, the Black Forest's largest stretch of water, entirely surrounded by fir-clad mountains. Here you can swim, windsurf or rent rowboats and sailing dinghies.

Titisee More crowded than the Schluchsee, but even more beautiful. It's also a favorite destination for swimmers and water-sports enthusiasts.

Heidelberg and the Neckar Valley

If any one city sums up Germany's romantic image it is Heidelberg. Seat of the country's oldest university and idyllically set astride the river Neckar, Heidelberg matches everyone's idea of a Germany of poets, painters, composers and thinkers. Composer Robert Schumann was a student at the university, Goethe fell in love here, every prominent name of the 19th-century German Romantic movement has sung Heidelberg's praises, in music and verse.

A walk through Heidelberg

Stroll down Heidelberg's main street, *Hauptstraße*, to the main square, the *Marktplatz*, passing the Old University, *Alte Universität*, founded in 1386 and rebuilt in the early 18th century. From *Marktplatz*, continue along *Kornmarkt* to the footpath which leads to Heidelberg's ruined castle, source of inspiration for German Romantic poets. Within the castle walls are two fascinating attractions: the *Apothekenmuseum*, basically a reconstruction of an 18th-century apothecary's shop, and the *Heidelberger Faß*, an enormous wine barrel made from 130 oak trees and capable of holding 49,000 gallons. You can save the long walk up to the castle by taking the *Königstuhl* funicular, which leaves at regular intervals from *Kornmarkt*.

Castles of the Neckar Valley

The road east from Heidelberg along the Neckar river is a central part of the *Burgenstraße* (Castle Road) tourist route. There are more castles on this stretch of the river than even the Rhine can boast.

Don't miss

Dilsberg, where unruly Heidelberg students were once incarcerated.
Schadeck, a complex of four castles above the picturesque riverside town of Neckarsteinach.
Hirschorn, now a stylish hotel and restaurant.
Zwingenberg, with a beautiful, frescoed 15th-century chapel.
Hornberg, 16th-century home of the legendary German knight Goetz von Berlichingen and now partly a hotel and restaurant, serving wines from the castle's own vineyards.
Bad Wimpfen, with remains of a palace built by the Emperor Barbarossa.

Franconia

Franconia (Franken) makes up the northern half of Bavaria, roughly the area between the Danube and Main rivers. But historically it's a proudly independent region, the ancient kingdom of the Franks. It contains some of the historically most important cities of Germany and villages of great charm and beauty. Its upland, heavily forested Fichtelgebirge area, bordering the Czech Republic, is a year-round attraction, offering a large network of hiking routes, ski trails and, on its highest slopes, reasonably

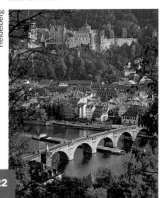

Heidelberg

challenging downhill runs. Franconia is also one of Germany's cheapest regions for tourists – and, as another recommendation, it has the largest concentration of local breweries, producing an almost limitless variety of beers.

Don't miss

Bamberg, an enchanting little city with a great history which reached its peak under the rule of the Holy Roman Emperor Heinrich II. He was crowned in 1003 in Bamberg cathedral, the Dom, which still dominates the city's steep-eaved skyline.

Bayreuth, the Wagnerian city, where the composer is honored every August with a festival of his operas. Tickets are very difficult to obtain, but tours are given daily of the opera house, the *Festspielhaus*, which the composer himself commissioned. That explains why the seating is so uncomfortable but the acoustics are so marvelous.

Coburg, another beautiful and historic Franconian city and home of the Saxe-Coburg-Gotha noble dynasty, whose members, over the centuries, have married into every European royal family. Queen Victoria's consort, Prince Albert, spent much of his childhood in Coburg's huge ducal palace, Schloß Ehrenburg.

Nürnberg, or Nuremberg as this great center of German history and culture is known in English. The city, 90 percent destroyed in the Second World War, is a model of reconstruction, with its beautifully restored medieval streets dominated by the brooding presence of the

rebuilt imperial castle, the *Kaiserburg*, residence of several rulers of the Holy Roman Empire. Nürnberg was the home of the German Renaissance painter Albrecht Dürer from 1509 until his death in 1528, and the house where he lived (Albrecht-Dürer-Straße 39) can be visited. A less pleasant reminder of Nürnberg's past history is the vast *Zeppelinfeld*, on the eastern edge of the city, where Hitler addressed the Nazi rallies.

The Bavarian Forest

This remote area of eastern Bavaria stretches north from the river Danube to the borders of the Czech Republic, where it joins the Bohemian Forest to become one of the largest and wildest woodland regions in all Europe. It's a nature-lover's paradise, where nearly every village is well off the beaten track and joined to the next by picturesque paths and ski trails. Its only city, Passau, is beautifully located, at the confluence of three rivers, two of which – the Danube and the Inn – hold the old town center in an affectionate embrace. The region is studded with "sport hotels" offering every kind of leisure activity at very reasonable rates, making the Bavarian Forest a favorite vacation destination for families.

Passau
Passau once held a position of power totally unrelated to its modest size. It was the seat of prince-bishops whose realm extended as far as Hungary. Their influence is witnessed by a collection of imposing buildings, including:
The Residenz, which today houses a museum containing the city's historic episcopal treasures.
The Veste Oberhaus, the city's original fortress, brooding over the old town center from a commanding

position above the river Danube. The view from its terraces is stunning.

The cathedral, or Dom, a mighty Baroque structure with the world's largest organ. Recitals are played on it at noon daily from May until the end of October.

The Allgäu and Bavarian Alps

Germany is separated from Austria in the extreme south by its highest range of mountains, the Allgäu Alps and the Bavarian Alps. They stretch in an almost unbroken chain of peaks from the Bodensee in the west to the remote southeastern corner of Germany around Berchtesgaden. It's an enchanting region of gradually ascending Alpine foothills, upland meadows and lakes, backed by fir-clad mountains and rocky peaks. Virtually every town and village here is a spa or ski resort.

Schloß Herrenchiemsee

Don't miss

Berchtesgaden, a busy Alpine market town forever linked with the name of its most famous visitor, Adolf Hitler. Bus tours run from the town center to the site of his "Eagle Nest" retreat, from where you can soak in the stunning Alpine views which so captivated the Führer.
Garmisch-Partenkirchen, the region's premier ski resort and site

of the 1936 Winter Olympics. The bustling town is at the foot of Germany's highest mountain, the 9,731ft Zugspitze. You can ride most of the way to the top on a cog railway, completing the journey in a cable car, or make the entire journey in a fraction of the time by cable car. Either way, a trip to the summit of the Zugspitze is a must.
Mittenwald, one of the prettiest Bavarian Alpine towns and a historic violin-making center. You can watch the violin-makers at work and, if the fancy takes you, have one made to order.
Oberammergau, the "Passion Play" town. The famous play is presented every ten years, with the next production scheduled for the year 2000. Daily tours are given of the Passion Play theater. Oberammergau is also a wood-carving center, and craftsmen appear to be at work all over town.

The Bavarian lakes
The Bavarian Alps are studded with beautiful lakes, fed mostly from mountain streams and springs. The loveliest are:
Chiemsee, Bavaria's largest lake, with two islands, on one of which King Ludwig II built the largest of his many palaces. (See below.)
Königsee, tucked into the mountainous far eastern corner of the Bavarian Alps, where your boatman will sound a trumpet call to demonstrate the echo that bounces off the surrounding cliffs.
Tegernsee, the loveliest lake of all, ringed by mountains and with an

Lindau

ancient monastery where one of Bavaria's finest beers is served by hefty matrons in a huge, vaulted tavern, the Bräustüberl.

Ludwig's castles

Bavaria's "mad" King Ludwig II built three sumptuous castles or palaces in the Bavarian Alpine region, selecting sites of extraordinary natural beauty. The most extravagant and famous of them all is **Neuschwanstein,** whose fairy-castle towers and battlements seem to float above the rocky and forested face of the mountains near the village of Schwangau.

Schloß Linderhof stands in lonely splendor in a narrow valley between Garmisch-Partenkirchen and Oberammergau. It's the smallest but many say the most beautiful of Ludwig's palaces. It's certainly the one where he himself spent most time.

Schloß Herrenchiemsee, on an island of the Chiemsee lake, was modeled along the formal lines of Versailles, but was never finished. A boat runs regularly to the island from the village of Stock.

The Bodensee (Lake Constance)

This shimmering stretch of water, backed in the south by the Swiss Alpine range, is the largest lake in the German-speaking world. Switzerland and Austria share its shores, and the largest town on the lake, Konstanz, is partly Swiss. Two of its towns literally sit in the lake, at the end of causeways:

Lindau, originally three islands, developed by the Romans, whose presence is still visible in the harbor which survives intact. From the harbor lighthouse, the Neuer Leuchtturm, there's a fine view of the town, the lake and the mountains beyond.

Wasserburg, whose name – "water castle" – describes how the town first came to arise out there in the lake. The castle, built on the foundations of a Roman watchtower, is now a comfortable hotel, the Schloßhotel Wasserburg.

Other Bodensee towns and sights not to be missed include:

■ **Birnau,** a village dominated by its magnificent, 18th-century Rococo church, the Wallfahrtskirche, with a rich interior of dazzling beauty.

■ **Friedrichshafen,** where the first zeppelins were built. The story of the development of the airship is told in the Zeppelin-Museum Technik und Kunst.

■ **Konstanz,** saved because of its half-Swiss character from war-time bombing and consequently one of Germany's best-preserved medieval towns. The reformist theologian Jan Hus was executed here in 1415, and he is commemorated in various ways throughout the town.

■ **Meersburg,** an enchanting, ancient town which spills down a steep bank of the lake. It has Germany's oldest inhabited castle, with a fascinating display of old jousting equipment.

■ **The islands of Murnau and Reichenau.** Murnau is known as the "island of flowers," because of its profusion of cultivated exotic plants and shrubs, including Germany's only banana plantation. Reichenau has flowers, too, but is better known for its unique collection of three Romanesque churches, said by many to be the loveliest in Europe.

Schloß Linderhof

Austria

Post-war Austria (or Österreich, to give the country its proper German name) has managed to retain its political, economic and cultural identity despite the presence and steady growth of its mighty neighbor, Germany. The Austrian Habsburgs vigorously challenged Germany's Hohenzollerns and Wittelsbachs for control of Europe's German-speaking regions. Vienna was an imperial capital long before Berlin, and from its location on the river Danube it once ruled most of central Europe. But the country's pivotal position, sandwiched between East and West, also made it a European battlefield, and its borders were overrun many times by invading armies. Austria is proud to have stopped the Turks in one of these campaigns, claiming to have rescued Western Europe from Turkish dominance. Vienna still has the feel of a city at the crossroads of East and West, and many Austrians adhere to the popular saying that "Vienna is where East thinks it's West, and vice versa." There are still areas of misunderstanding between Austria and neighboring Germany, but they are mostly confined to popular misconceptions and prejudices. You can meet German motorists who seriously maintain that Austrian traffic police keep a specially sharp eye out for them, while in some Austrian resorts German visitors are treated with noticeable coolness. Nevertheless, this is where German Chancellor Helmut Kohl chose to spend his summer vacations and regular spa sessions, and millions of Germans follow his lead. Austria is totally geared to tourism, from the cultural festivals of Vienna, Salzburg and Innsbruck to the winter sports programs of its Alpine resorts, the summer seasons of its lovely lakes and the wine festivals of its vineyard villages. Like Switzerland, it's not a cheap vacation destination, but it offers good value for money and very high standards.

Johann Strauss, Stadt Park, Vienna

Vienna

Vienna (Wien) is much more than Austria's stately capital, it's the very essence of the country. The grand imperial buildings that dominate the city center proclaim the glory of its Habsburg past, while there's a commanding dignity about its people that bears quiet witness to their proud history. Horse-drawn open carriages compete for custom with taxis, and the clatter of hooves on cobbled streets adds to the evocative music that is never absent for long in Vienna. The slow pace of

Viennese life is typified by its famous coffeehouse routine, where business deals are sealed and liaisons arranged at dark oak tables cluttered with fine china and pastries. It's an aging city, in every sense, with a larger proportion of over-60s than any other in Europe. At the turn of the century it was the world's fourth largest city, but its population of two million has since declined by one quarter. Yet visit Vienna in summer and you'll find a city of youthful vigor and gaiety, with champagne bars doing roaring business in its central, pedestrians-only streets.

In the depths of winter – which can be a grim, dank time – social life moves inside, into restaurants with history written on their paneled walls and *Wiener Schnitzel* – Austria's great contribution to the culinary world – written large on virtually every menu.

Don't miss

A stroll through Josefsplatz, where much of "The Third Man" was filmed.

Sunday morning mass, hauntingly sung in Latin, at the 14th-century Augustinerkirche.

A visit to the Albertina museum, which has the world's largest collection of drawings, sketches, engravings and etchings.

A tour of the Hofburg, the former royal palace, where you can see the imperial apartments of Emperor Franz Josef and Empress Elisabeth, as well as some fascinating personal items (including the dress she was wearing when stabbed to death by an Italian anarchist on the shores of Lake Geneva in 1898).

Salzburg

A performance at the Wiener Staatsoper, the city's famous and magnificent opera house, if you're lucky enough to secure a ticket. If luck is out, settle for one of the tours given at regular intervals.

A visit to Vienna's great cathedral, the Stephansdom, with its strikingly colorful tile roof, added in the 19th century. If you're up to it, climb the 345 steps of the Alte Steffl tower, for a fine panoramic view of the city.

Schönbrunn Palace A 15-minute ride from the city center (on the U-4 subway), the baroque residence of the Habsburgs is an essential part of a Vienna tourist itinerary.

Cafés and restaurants

Demel, Kohlmarkt 14, Vienna's justifiably most famous and best-loved coffeehouse and restaurant, with divine pastries and an imaginative lunch menu.

Landtmann, Dr.-Karl-Lueger-Ring 4, a favorite of Sigmund Freud and later Marlene Dietrich, who loved its discreet, curtained-off seclusion. Famous players from the nearby Burgtheater are regulars there.

Mozart, Albertinaplatz 2, where Orson Welles took breaks from filming "The Third Man."

Zu den Drei Husaren, Weihburg-gasse 4, a Viennese institution, where you dine by candlelight and to the accompaniment of a grand piano.

Salzburg

Mozart's birthplace is an enchanting small city straddling a fast-flowing river, the Salzach, which gathers its waters from the nearby mountains. It's dominated by a grim fortress, with battlements and dungeons, and crisscrossed by narrow streets lined by some of Austria's most exclusive boutiques. The Alpine meadows of "The Sound of Music" are a bike ride away, and some of Austria's prettiest lakes are also near at hand.

Don't miss

A pilgrimage to Mozart's birthplace, now a museum dedicated to the city's most famous son, Getreidegasse 9.

A stroll through the Mirabell Gardens to the baroque Schloß Mirabell.

An excursion to Schloß Hellbrunn, about three miles outside Salzburg (on bus number 55), a 16th-century palace built for the city's powerful prince-bishops.

The Austrian Alps

The Austrian Alps stretch from the Swiss frontier more than 125 miles eastwards to the Carinthian peaks bordering Slovenia. They offer some of Europe's most challenging skiing but also contain picturesque mountain resorts ideal for family vacations, in winter and in summer. The main Alpine regions and resorts are:

Vorarlberg (with fashionable St. Anton at its center); the **Tirol** (Innsbruck, Mayrhofen, Gerlos); **Osttirol** (the Eastern Tyrol, where Austria's two highest mountains, the Großvenediger and the Groß-glockner brood over the region); the

Salzburger Alpen (St. Johann, Kitzbühel), the wild **Steiermark** and **Kärnten** (Carinthia, whose lovely lakes make this region a favored summer vacation destination as well as a region for winter sports enthusiasts).

Information on winter vacations in Austria can be obtained from:
Winterwelt Österreich, Kongresszentrum Seeburg, A-9210 Pörtschach, tel. 04272/362035.

Eating out in Austria

Because of its central European location, Austria has developed a cuisine that runs from Bohemian and Hungarian to distinctly southern Italian. In fact, the Italians claim the *Wiener Schnitzel* was originally a Milan dish. Austrian variations of Hungarian goulash are often better than the original, while the German staple *Tafelspitz* (boiled beef) has been refined and improved by the Austrians. In Vienna, the Jewish tradition lives on in the kitchens of the Beisln, inexpensive and hospitable taverns. On the outskirts of the city – and particularly in the romantic Wienerwald forest – *Heurige* (young wine) taverns offer new wine and traditional dishes with often a gypsy orchestra thrown in for good measure.

Getting around Austria

By air
Austrian Airlines operate international flights to and from Vienna and internal services between Vienna, Linz, Salzburg, Graz and Innsbruck. Fares, however, are expensive.

By car
Austria has a German-style *Autobahn* network, connecting Vienna with the southern cities of Graz and Klagenfurt and with Salzburg and Innsbruck (via southern Germany) in the west. There are no tolls, except for the *Autobahn* linking southern Austria and Northern Italy via the Brenner pass.

By train
The rail network in Austria is extensive, connecting Vienna and outlying cities with hourly, InterCity services and penetrating deep into the Alps. There are ten privately-operated lines, two of them (*Achenseebahn* and *Zillertalbahn*) still using steam locomotives. There are various reduced fare offers, chief of which are the *Bundesnetzkarte*, offering unlimited travel for a month, and the *Österreich Puzzle* ticket, covering travel in up to four special zones.

Accommodations

Austria differs little from neighboring Germany in the range, quality and price category of its hotels, *Pensions* and country inns. All the major international hotel chains are represented in Vienna, Salzburg and Innsbruck. In rural regions such as Lower Austria overnight accommodations can be surprisingly cheap, usually including a substantial buffet breakfast. In the mountain resorts the range of accommodation is vast, from luxurious establishments of Grand Hotel style to simple farmhouse rooms. Most resorts have a virtually year-round season (usually falling sharply in November), and each has its own tourist office where reservations can be made.

Buying things

Austria has a long wood-carving tradition. You'll find wood-carvers at work in many mountain villages and examples of their craft are to be found in city boutiques and also in the department stores. The Austrian mountains also produce fine *Bergkristall*, that ice-like, sharply cut crystal. Small crystals can be bought in city markets for a few Schillings, but for more substantial examples you'll have to go to specialist shops or jewelers. Handmade Austrian jewelry, particularly wrought gold, is of high quality. The goldsmiths of Linz are held in particularly high esteem. Visitors with a sweet tooth will pounce on Salzburg's famous specialty, the *Mozartkugeln*, delicious chocolate and marzipan truffles.

the Golden Roof, Innsbruck

Useful telephone numbers
- **Police:** 133
- **Ambulance:** 144
- **Fire Department:** 122
- **Train schedule information:** 1717

Holidays, festivals and events

Vienna Haydn-Tage (Haydn Festival), March; Frühlingsfestival (Spring music festival), April/May; Festwochen (theater festival), May/June; Wiener Musik-Sommer (music festival), June – September; Donauinselfest (rock and pop festival), June; Jazzfest, July; Internationale Tanzwochen Wien (dance festival), July/August; Schubert-Festival, November; Mozart-Festival, December; Adventzauber (Christmas market), late November – Christmas Eve.

Innsbruck Festwochen der Alten Musik (Festival of Ancient Music), August; Innsbrucker Sommer (theater, music and dance festival), June – October; Christkindlmarkt (Christmas market), late November – December 22.

Salzburg Salzburger Mozartwoche (Salzburg Mozart week), late January – early February; Salzburger Festspiele (music festival), July/August; Christkindlmarkt (Christmas market), late November – Christmas Eve.

Adventzauber, Vienna

German-speaking Switzerland

Many visitors to Switzerland maintain German isn't spoken there at all, so strange is the dialect of the eastern region designated as "German-speaking." It's called *Schwyzerdütsch*, and even Germans from just across the border find it hard to understand. It's certainly one of the facets of Switzerland that distinguish it so completely from Germany and its other German-speaking neighbor, Austria. German – or the *Schwyzerdütsch* dialect – is spoken by 65 percent of the country's 6.7 million inhabitants. The capital, Bern, and the country's two largest cities, Zürich and Basel, are all predominantly German-speaking.

Switzerland's history is closely linked with Germany's. The Swiss are of Celtic origin, tracing their roots back to the Helvetian tribe which settled in the region around 450 BC. In the eleventh

Zürich, the River Limmat and the Zürichsee

century most of present-day Switzerland was absorbed into the Holy Roman Empire of German Nations. In 1291 three communities formed the structure that was to serve as Switzerland's political system for several centuries: the *Eidgenossenschaft*, an economic and defense alliance which grew so strong that in 1386 it won a war against Austria. The region was plunged again into war during the Reformation, led by Zwingli and Calvin. In time the *Eidgenossenschaft* gave way to the Helvetian Republic, and in 1848 the country took its present form with the creation of a Federal State complete with federal constitution.

The 1848 constitution enshrines Switzerland's principle of neutrality, which it maintained through both world wars and which today gives the Swiss some cause for concern because of the country's central position within a rapidly uniting Europe. Its neutral stand has served Switzerland well, however, for today it's the world's second most prosperous country, with rock-like political stability and a currency so strong that it's virtually become the international reserve monetary system.

Its legendary reputation as a financial center out of all proportion to its size has its disadvantages, though. Zürich, for instance, has to contend with its popular image as a dour city of banks and insurance offices. In fact, it's a charming city, full of the contrasts that make Switzerland as a whole, and the German-speaking region in particular, such an interesting destination. The Alpine peaks, ski slopes, lush upland meadows and lovely lakes make up the tourist board Switzerland, but the discerning visitor will find a country with much more to offer.

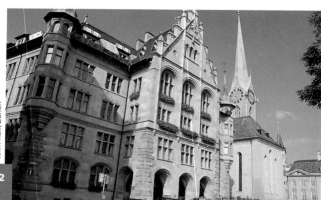

town hall, Zürich

Zürich

First-time visitors to Zürich, expecting a sleek financial metropolis, are almost invariably pleasantly surprised to find a compact lakeside city of old-fashioned charm. The banking institutions on which the city's economy rests are difficult to overlook, but they haven't taken over the cobbled backstreets of the old town. Most of these streets end at the water's edge, on the banks of the Limmat river which flows into the Zürichsee lake. Much of the city embraces the western end of the lake, which is a natural playground for the leisure-loving Swiss. Beyond the water to the south rise the majestic Swiss Alps, while northward stretch the lush meadows grazed by cows whose milk gives Swiss dairy products and chocolate their unmatchable quality.

Zürich is a city of churches.

Don't miss

Fraumünster, 13th century and with modern stained-glass windows by Marc Chagall.
Großmünster, founded by Charlemagne in the ninth century and from whose pulpit the reformer Huldrych Zwingli delivered some of his most heretical sermons.
Peterskirche, the city's oldest parish church, dating from the 13th century and bearing Europe's largest clockface.
Wasserkirche (the Water Church), a fine example of late Gothic church architecture.
The Kunsthaus, with a collection of works by artists of the Dadaist movement, which was founded in Zürich.
The Schweizerisches Landesmuseum, with exhibits illustrating Swiss history and a unique collection of Romanesque and pre-Romanesque ecclesiastical art.

The Alps: Zermatt and the Matterhorn

Switzerland's highest mountain is the 1,520ft Dufourspitze, but it's a neighboring one, the Matterhorn, which is the country's most famous peak. While the Dufourspitze is part of a mountain chain that rings the beautiful Alpine resort of Zermatt, the 1,469ft Matterhorn stands in splendid isolation. Both are best accessed from Zermatt, and guides can be hired from the tourist office, the Verkehrsbüro Zermatt, on Bahnhofsplatz, tel. 028-661181.

Zermatt bans private cars, which adds greatly to the small town's appeal. Don't miss a visit to its churchyard, where you'll find the graves of three members of the ill-fated Edward Whymper conquest of the Matterhorn. Whymper and his team were the first to climb the Matterhorn, in 1865, but on the ascent four of the team plunged to their deaths. The body of the fourth climber was never found.

German is spoken in the major part of Switzerland's spectacular Alpine region. In some of the more remote areas non-native German speakers might have difficulty understanding the local dialect, but the local inhabitants invariably understand "high German." The

the Matterhorn

Swiss Alps, by the way, are not just skiing territory – in summer and fall they are terrain for serious hikers, climbers or leisurely walkers. The major German-speaking Alpine regions and their principal resorts and most famous mountains are:

Berner Oberland Grindelwald, Gstaad, Lenk, Mürren, Wengen. The region that best sums up the enchantment of the Swiss Alps, with three of Switzerland's most celebrated mountains: the Eiger, Mönch and Jungfrau peaks. Information: Berner Oberland Tourismus, Jungfraustraße 38, CH-3800 Interlaken, tel. 41-33-823 0303, fax: 41-33-823 0330.

Graubünden Arosa, Davos, Klosters, Scuol, St. Moritz, Vals. Information: Verkehrsverein Graubünden, Alexanderstraße 24, CH-7001 Chur, tel. 41-81-302-6100, fax: 41-81-302 1414.

Ostschweiz/Liechtenstein: Braunwald, Malbun, St. Gallen. Information: Tourismusverband Ostschweiz, Bahnhofplatz 1a, CH-9001 St Gallen, tel. 41-71-227 3737, fax: 41-71-227 3767.

Wallis: Aletsch glacier, Crans-Montana, Saas Fee, Zermatt (at the foot of the Matterhorn). Information: Walliser Verkehrsverband, Postfach 919, CH-1950 Sitten, tel. 41-27-322 31 61, fax: 41-27-323 1572.

Zentralschweiz: Andermatt am Gotthard, Einsiedeln, Engelberg, Melchsee-Frutt, Rigi. Information: Zentralschweiz-Tourismus, Alpenstraße 1, CH-6002 Luzern, tel. 41-41-410 1891, fax: 41-41-410 7260.

Getting around

By air

Zürich is the main airport for the German-speaking region of Switzerland. Both Basel and Bern have smaller airports. Swissair has services to all of them, although most internal flights are operated by the company Crossair.

By road

Switzerland has an excellent highway network, maintained partly by a special tax on vehicles using it. The levy (30 Swiss Francs in 1996) buys a small vignette which has to be displayed on the windshield, and is valid for 14 months. It can be purchased at border crossings, most highway gas stations and at all tourist offices. There are speed limits of 75mph on highways, 50mph on normal roads and 19mph in built-up areas. Road service can be obtained by calling 140. Most mountain passes are closed to traffic in winter.

By train

The punctuality of Swiss trains is legendary. Service is swift and frequent, even in country areas. A "Swiss Travel System" pass is valid for unlimited travel on all trains, post buses, lake steamers and municipal transport systems in 25 cities and towns for a period of one month, four, eight or 15 days.

Food and drink

Switzerland's French- and Italian-speaking regions are the natural home of the country's haute cuisine, but the German-language area nevertheless manages to maintain a highly individual and high-quality tradition. Cheese raclette and fondue need no introduction, but other dishes to try include:

Käseschnitte, a casserole of oven-baked bread, cheese and ham
Pizokel, tiny, pasta-like dumplings
Maluns, pasta-filled cabbage
Rösti, Switzerland's inimitable version of fried potatoes

Beer and wine Switzerland's German-speaking region has a beer tradition to compare with Germany's own, and most towns and many villages have their local brewery. South-facing vineyards produce a wine of surprisingly high standard.

Useful telephone numbers
- **Police:** 117
- **Medical aid and Fire Dept.:** 118
- **Road service:** 140
- **Schweizerische Verkehrszentrale** – the Swiss national tourist office – is in Zürich: Bellariastraße 38, tel. 01-288 1111.
- **Train information:** 157 2222

Accommodations

The Swiss hotel trade is renowned for its efficiency and friendly service. The country has some of Europe's leading hotel training schools, whose graduates are to be found practicing those traditional Swiss virtues in cities and resorts throughout the world. Literature, stage and screen celebrate the leisurely, luxurious style of the fin-de-siècle Grand Hotels that are to be found on every Swiss lake. They are usually extremely expensive but offer an understated standard of elegance, comfort and unobtrusive service that the international chain hotels (also well represented in Switzerland) find hard to match. Many of the finest Grand Hotels are members of the Swiss Leading Hotels Group, which has a centralized reservation service. At the other end of the range are the small country hotels, *Pensions* and farmhouses that offer reasonably priced accommodations in often breathtakingly beautiful settings. (Zürich has a special telephone number for hotel reservations: 01-211-1131.)

Buying things

A cuckoo clock from Switzerland is, of course, the obvious souvenir, but any Swiss-made precision timepiece is guaranteed to be a good buy. Antique Swiss-made clocks and watches are a real investment, and the Basler Herbstmesse (fall exhibition from late October until mid-November) is the place to strike gold. Swiss-made jewellery, lace and silk clothing (shirts and lingerie, for instance) are of guaranteed high quality, although expensive.

Zürich

Holidays, festivals and events

Zürich Sechseläuten (spring festival) mid-April; Theaterspektakel am See (open-air theater festival) mid-August until mid-September; Jazz Festival, early July; Weihnachtsmarkt (Christmas market) late November until Christmas Eve
Basel Basler Fasnacht (Basel Carnival) late February; Casino Jazz Festival, late August; Weihnachtsmarkt (Christmas market) early December until 23 December

Basler Fasnacht

Bare necessities

Greetings

Hello!	**Hallo!**
Good day/morning/evening!	**Guten Tag/Morgen/Abend!**
How are you?	**Wie geht's?** (informal)/**Wie geht es Ihnen?** (formal)
Good, thank you.	**Gut, danke.**
Goodbye!	**Auf Wiedersehen!** (formal)/**Tschüß!** (informal)
See you (soon/tomorrow).	**Bis bald/morgen.**
May I introduce Mr./Mrs./Ms. . . .	**Darf ich vorstellen? Herr/Frau . . .**
Nice to meet you!	**Angenehm!** (formal)/**Freut mich!** (less formal)

Other useful words

yes/no	**ja/nein**
Thanks a lot.	**Vielen Dank/Danke schön.**
Of course.	**Natürlich/Selbstverständlich.**
You're welcome.	**Bitte schön.**
Excuse me/Sorry.	**Entschuldigung.**
Sorry.	**Tut mir leid/Entschuldigung.**
Excuse me?	**Wie bitte?**
You're welcome.	**Keine Ursache.**
Please/Here you are.	**Bitte/Bitte schön.**
It's very (nice/interesting).	**Es ist sehr (schön/interessant).**

Is / are there . . . ?

Is/are there (a pharmacy/a hotel/a bus/a concert/an elevator/any restrooms) here?	**Gibt es hier (eine Apotheke/ ein Hotel/einen Bus/ ein Konzert/ einen Fahrstuhl/ Toiletten)?**

Where is / are . . . ?

Excuse me, where is (the station/town center)?	**Entschuldigung, wo ist (der Bahnhof/das Zentrum)?**
On the right/left/straight ahead.	**Rechts/links/geradeaus.**
That is here/there.	**Das ist hier/dort.**

Wohin möchten Sie?	Where would you like to go?
Hier geradeaus.	Here straight ahead.
Tut mir leid. Ich weiß nicht.	I'm sorry. I don't know.
Eine/zwei Stunden.	One/two hours.

Do you have any . . . ?

What is that called?	**Wie heißt das?**
Do you have (a table/a double room/batteries/toothpaste)?	**Haben Sie (einen Tisch/ein Doppelzimmer/Batterien/ Zahnpasta)?**

How much . . . ?

How much is (the ticket/ the room/the CD)?	**Was kostet (die Karte/ das Zimmer/die CD)?**
How much is that altogether?	**Wieviel macht das zusammen?**

I'd like . . .

I'd like (a ticket/ a kilo of apples).	**Ich möchte (eine Karte/ein Kilo Äpfel).**

Getting things straight

I don't understand!	**Ich verstehe nicht!**
I only speak a little German.	**Ich spreche nur ein bißchen Deutsch.**
Once again, please.	**Noch einmal, bitte.**
Slowly, please.	**Langsam, bitte.**
Do you understand?	**Verstehen Sie?** (formal)/ **Verstehst du?** (informal)
Do you speak English?	**Sprechen Sie Englisch?**
Please spell it.	**Bitte buchstabieren Sie.**
Please write it down.	**Bitte schreiben Sie es auf.**
What does . . . mean?	**Was bedeutet . . . ?**
I don't know.	**Ich weiß nicht.**

About yourself

My name is . . .	**Ich heiße . . ./Mein Name ist . . .**
I'm from the United States.	**Ich komme aus Vereinigte Staaten.**
I'm on vacation.	**Ich mache Urlaub.**
I'm on a business trip.	**Ich bin auf Geschäftsreise.**
I'm a student.	**Ich bin Student/Studentin.**
I have (two/three/no) children).	**Ich habe (zwei/drei/keine) Kinder.**
(see p41 for nationalities)	

About other people

What is your name?	**Wie heißen Sie?** (formal)
Where are you from?	**Woher kommen Sie?** (formal)
Are you on vacation?	**Machen Sie hier Urlaub?**
How do you like it?	**Wie gefällt es Ihnen?**
What do you do?	**Was sind Sie von Beruf?**

Money

The currency in Germany is referred to as the Mark, abbreviated as DM.

prices	**Preise**
3,45 DM	**drei Mark fünfundvierzig**
56,00 DM	**sechsundfünfzig Mark**
check	**Scheck**
(see p40 for numbers)	

Changing money

I'd like to (change some money/ exchange some traveler's checks/pay by credit card).	**Ich möchte (Geld tauschen/ Reiseschecks einlösen/ mit Kreditkarte bezahlen).**
What is the exchange rate today?	**Wie ist der Kurs heute?**
Do you take commission?	**Nehmen Sie Kommission?**
What's the commission charge?	**Wieviel ist die Kommission?**

Geldautomat

Some common quantities

ein Pfennig	0,01 DM
fünf Pfennig	0,05 DM
zehn Pfennig	0,10 DM
fünfzehn Pfennig	0,15 DM
eine Mark	1,00 DM
zwei Mark	2,00 DM
fünf Mark	5,00 DM
zehn Mark	10,00 DM
zwanzig Mark	20,00 DM
fünfzig Mark	50,00 DM
einhundert Mark	100,00 DM

Changing money

fünfzig Dollars	fifty dollars
Wie steht Der Dollar?	What is the dollar at?
Der Dollar steht bei zwei Mark dreißig.	The dollar is at 1,88 DM.

The time

What time is it?	**Wie spät ist es?**
What time does the performance start?	**Wann beginnt die Vorstellung?**
When does the train leave?	**Wann fährt der Zug ab?**
from . . . till	**von . . . bis**

Wie lange (sind Sie hier/möchten Sie bleiben)?	How long (are you here for/would you like to stay)?
beginnt/fährt um . . .	starts/leaves at . . .
acht Uhr	8:00
zehn nach acht	8:10
zehn vor acht	7:50
Viertel nach acht/acht Uhr fünfzehn	8:15
Viertel vor acht/sieben Uhr fünfundvierzig	7:45
halb acht/sieben Uhr dreißig	7.30

heute	today	**nachmittags**	in the afternoon
gestern	yesterday		
morgens	in the morning	**abends**	in the evening
vormittags	in the late morning	**nachts**	at night
		gestern Abend	yesterday evening
mittags	lunchtime		
		heute Morgen	this morning

Days of the week

Montag	Monday	**Freitag**	Friday
Dienstag	Tuesday	**Samstag**	Saturday
Mittwoch	Wednesday	**Sonntag**	Sunday
Donnerstag	Thursday		

Montag,Dienstag
Mittwoch,Freitag   9.30-20.00 Uhr
Donnerstag   10.00-20.00 Uhr
Samstag   10.00-16.00 Uhr

Months

Januar	January	**Juli**	July
Februar	February	**August**	August
März	March	**September**	September
April	April	**Oktober**	October
Mai	May	**November**	November
Juni	June	**Dezember**	December

Numbers

0	**null**	18	**achtzehn**
1	**eins**	19	**neunzehn**
2	**zwei**	20	**zwanzig**
3	**drei**	21	**einundzwanzig**
4	**vier**	22	**zweiundzwanzig**
5	**fünf**	23	**dreiundzwanzig**
6	**sechs**	30	**dreißig**
7	**sieben**	40	**vierzig**
8	**acht**	50	**fünfzig**
9	**neun**	60	**sechzig**
10	**zehn**	70	**siebzig**
11	**elf**	80	**achtzig**
12	**zwölf**	90	**neunzig**
13	**dreizehn**	100	**einhundert**
14	**vierzehn**	200	**zweihundert**
15	**fünfzehn**	315	**dreihundert-**
16	**sechzehn**		**fünfzehn**
17	**siebzehn**		

Understanding the system

The numbers are not as complicated as you may think. All you have to do is to learn the numbers from one to twelve. The teens following twelve are just combined of those + the ending **-zehn**. For example: 14 is **vierzehn**, meaning four + ten.
The numbers over 20 work as follows: 21 is **einundzwanzig**, meaning one and 20.

Colors

blau	blue
braun	brown
gelb	yellow
grün	green
orange	orange
rot	red
schwarz	black
weiß	white

Countries and nationalities
Country: adjective, inhabitant

America	**Amerika: amerikanisch, Amerikaner/in**
Australia	**Australien: australisch, Australier/in**
Austria	**Österreich: österreichisch, Österreicher/in**
Belgium	**Belgien: belgisch, Belgier/in**
Canada	**Kanada: kanadisch, Kanadier/in**
China	**China: chinesisch, Chinese/Chinesin**
Denmark	**Dänemark: dänisch, Däne/Dänin**
England	**England: englisch, Engländer/in**
Finland	**Finnland: finnisch, Finne/Finnin**
France	**Frankreich: französisch, Franzose/Französin**
Germany	**Deutschland: deutsch, Deutscher/Deutsche**
Greece	**Griechenland: griechisch, Grieche/Griechin**
India	**Indien: indisch, Inder/in**
Ireland	**Irland: irländisch, Ire/Irin**
Italy	**Italien: italienisch, Italiener/in**
Japan	**Japan: japanisch, Japaner/in**
Korea	**Korea: koreanisch, Koreaner/in**
Luxembourg	**Luxemburg: luxemburgisch, Luxemburger/in**
Netherlands	**Holland: holländisch/niederländisch, Holländer/in**
New Zealand	**Neuseeland: neuseeländisch, Neuseeländer/in**
Northern Ireland	**Nordirland: nordirländisch, Nordire/Nordirin**
Norway	**Norwegen: norwegisch, Norweger/in**
Portugal	**Portugal: portugiesisch, Portugiese/Portugiesin**
Russia	**Rußland: russisch, Russe/Russin**
Scotland	**Schottland: schottisch, Schotte/Schottin**
South Africa	**Südafrika: südafrikanisch, Südafrikaner/in**
Spain	**Spanien: spanisch, Spanier/in**
Sweden	**Schweden: schwedisch, Schwede/Schwedin**
Switzerland	**Schweiz: schweizerisch, Schweizer/in**
United States	**Vereinigte Staaten: amerikanisch, Amerikaner/in**
Wales	**Wales: walisisch, Waliser/in**

Alphabet

In German the letters of the alphabet are pronounced as follows.

A (ah)	H (hah)	O (oh)	V (fow)
B (bay)	I (ee)	P (pay)	W (vah)
C (tse)	J (yot)	Q (cou)	X (eks)
D (day)	K (kah)	R (arh)	Y (epsilon)
E (ay)	L (al)	S (as)	Z (tsat)
F (af)	M (am)	T (tay)	
G (gay)	N (an)	U (oo)	

(for further pronunciation see Sounds German at the back of the book)

Sound Check

Entschuldigung is a long word, which has the stress on the second syllable: ant-chool-de-goong

Zentrum: the "z" is a sharp sound like the "ts" in "cats"

Language works

Meeting people

1 Introducing oneself
■ **Guten Morgen.**
□ **Guten Morgen. Ich bin Jens Bahlke. Wie heißen Sie?**
■ **Ich heiße Sarah Callingham.**
□ **Machen Sie hier Urlaub?**
■ **Ja, für zwei Wochen.**
□ **Wie gefällt es Ihnen?**
■ **Es ist sehr interessant.**

How long is the guest on vacation? Does she like it?

2 More talk
■ **Guten Tag. Wie geht es Ihnen?**
□ **Sehr gut, danke.**
■ **Mein Name ist Collins. Darf ich vorstellen . . . meine Frau.**
□ **Angenehm.**
■ **Angenehm.**
□ **Woher kommen Sie?**
■ **Aus Sydney, Australien.**

Frau Collins is your: sister/wife/mother.
You're from Australia: true/false

3 Finding your way
■ **Entschuldigung, gibt es hier einen Bus?**
□ **Wohin möchten Sie?**
■ **Zum Bahnhof, bitte.**
□ **Hier geradeaus.**
■ **Vielen Dank.**

Where do you find a bus?

4 Trying to make sense of it
■ **Wie bitte? Ich verstehe nicht.**
□ **Wurst mit Salat.**
■ **Ich spreche nur ein bißchen Deutsch. Sprechen Sie Englisch?**
□ **Natürlich. Sausage with salad.**

What do you ask the waiter?

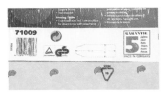

Try it out

As if you were there

Find out about somebody in an informal way
■ (Say hello and ask how that person is)
□ **Hallo. Gut, danke.**
■ (Ask that person's name)
□ **Ich heiße Susanne. Und wie heißt du?**
■ (Say your name and ask where Susanne is from)
□ **Ich komme aus Jena. Woher kommst du?**
■ (Say where you are from)

Numbers

Who has got these lottery numbers?
Claudia Hauswirt 16 13 03
    Christel Ahlf 06 51 95
Peter Wiese 50 11 43
    Ruth Städing 17 13 12
Volker Bruns 16 73 12
    Britta Nessel 81 20 65

a **siebzehn dreizehn zwölf ?**
b **fünfzig elf dreiundvierzig?**
c **sechzehn dreizehn null drei?**

Getting around

By air

Germany's biggest air carrier, Lufthansa, connects all cities with virtually round-the-clock services. Air travel within Germany, however, is expensive, and even special *Flieg und Spar* (Fly and Save) tariffs are far dearer than train travel. Deutsche BA offers some cheapies, mostly to and from Berlin. The carrier LTU, based in Düsseldorf, has a last-minute schedule offering big savings on flights between its Rhineland airport and major cities such as Berlin, Hamburg and Munich.

By boat

Regular boat services ply not only the Rhine but other rivers such as the Danube, Elbe, Main and Moselle. The main operator is the KD company. German Railways, the Deutsche Bahn, operate ferry services on Lake Constance, the Bodensee, while privately run pleasure boat services are found on every lake of any size.

By bus

The nearest Germany has to a national bus network are the tourist route services offered by Deutsche Touring. Special long-distance buses, with guide, cover some of Germany's most popular tourist routes, such as the Romantic Road (*Romantische Straße*). Daily bus services also connect Berlin with most major cities. For schedules and fares contact Deutsche Touring, Am Römerhof 17, 60426 Frankfurt/Main, tel. 069/79030. Most country districts have bus services run by private operators or the German Railways, the *Deutsche Bahn*, but they are usually patchy and irregular.

> Where is the bus station, please?
> **Wo ist der Busbahnhof, bitte?**

By car

Germany's autobahns are legendary, of course, and justifiably so. The country is covered by a comprehensive highway network totaling thousands of miles. There are no tolls; that's a mixed blessing, though, for toll-free driving leads to very crowded autobahns. Gas stations and drive-in restaurant services are to be found every 30 miles or so. Gas prices at autobahn stops, however, tend to be considerably more expensive than at off-highway sites, so it can pay to leave the autobahn to fill up at the nearest village pump. Germany's main automobile club, the ADAC, comes to the assistance of motorists in need of roadside help, charging only the cost of repairs, parts or towing. Assistance telephones are positioned at one-and-a-half-mile intervals.

Car rental

All major car rental firms (Avis, Budget, Europcar, Hertz) have offices at airports and city railway stations. A national driver's license and passport are the only documents required, while credit cards are the preferred method of payment.

❗ I'd like to rent a car, please.
● Ich möchte ein Auto mieten.

Train travel

The privatized German Railways (*Deutsche Bahn*) are a European model of how to run a rail service. Their countrywide network serves even the smallest communities, while the ultra high-speed *InterCity Express* (ICE) can compete with the airlines on some of its routes (Munich–Frankfurt, for instance). Between the two types of service is a comprehensive range of customized trains: the *InterCity* (slower and cheaper than the InterCity Express), the *EuroCity* (connecting German cities with destinations abroad), the *InterRegio* (for travel within specific regions), the slow D-trains (with sleeper services between cities) and the short-distance E-trains.

❗ A round-trip ticket to Munich, please.
● Nach München, hin und zürück, bitte.

A hotel-on-wheels service is being developed, with Berlin as the main destination. It's the last word in sleeper comfort, offering passengers the chance of dining aboard the train before it departs and breakfast in bed. The *Deutsche Bahn* has a wide range of special ticket offers, which changes with confusing frequency. The all-time favorite, however, is the German Rail Pass, available for periods of five, ten or 15 days. It also allows travel on lake ferries operated by the *Deutsche Bahn*.

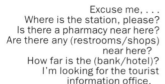

Phrasemaker
Finding the way

Excuse me, . . .	**Entschuldigung, . . .**
Where is the station, please?	**Wo ist der Bahnhof, bitte?**
Is there a pharmacy near here?	**Gibt es hier eine Apotheke?**
Are there any (restrooms/shops) near here?	**Gibt es hier in der Nähe (Toiletten/Geschäfte)?**
How far is the (bank/hotel)?	**Wie weit ist (die Bank/das Hotel)?**
I'm looking for the tourist information office.	**Ich suche die Touristen-information.**
Is the (cathedral/market) far from here?	**Ist (die Kathedrale/der Markt) weit von hier?**
Is this the right way to the (bus station/town center/market square)?	**Ist dies der Weg zum (Busbahnhof/Stadtzentrum/Marktplatz)?**

rechts/links/geradeaus	right/left/straight ahead
auf der (rechten/linken) Seite	on the (right/left)
(an der/um die) Ecke	(at the/around the) corner
Sie (gehen/fahren)	you (go/drive)
die (nächste/erste/zweite) Straße	the (next/first/second) street
zweihundert Meter/Kilometer	200 meters/kilometers
am Ende der Straße	at the end of the street
hier/da	here/there
bis	as far as
über (die Brücke/die Straße)	across the (bridge/street)
Es ist ziemlich (weit/nah).	It is fairly (far/close).
bei/gegenüber/hinter/vor/neben	near/opposite/behind/in front of/next to

Places to look for

die Altstadt	the old part of the town	**die Kirche**	church
die Apotheke	pharmacy	**das Kranken-haus**	hospital
die Autobahn	highway	**der Markt**	market
der Bahnhof	station	**der Marktplatz**	market square
die Bank	bank	**die Messe**	fair
die Bushalte-stelle	bus stop	**das Museum**	museum
		der Park	park
das Einkaufs-zentrum	shopping center	**der Platz**	square
		das Schloß	castle
der Flughafen	airport	**das Schwimm-bad**	swimming pool
das Fremden-verkehrsbüro	tourist office		
		der See	lake
das Geschäft	store	**das Stadion**	stadium
der Hafen	port	**die Straße**	street
die Innenstadt	city center	**die Toilette**	restroom

Pedestrian signs

(rechts/links) sehen	look (right/left)
Kreuzung	crossing
Fußgängerzone	pedestrian zone
Fahrradweg	bicycle path

Renting a car or bike

Ausfahrt

I'd like to rent a (car/bike), please.	**Ich möchte bitte (ein Auto mieten/ein Fahrrad leihen).**
For (three days/one week)	**Für (drei Tage/eine Woche)**
How much is it per (day/week)?	**Was kostet das pro (Tag/Woche)?**
Is insurance included?	**Versicherung inklusive?**
small/fairly large	**klein/ziemlich groß**

Ihren Führerschein, bitte.	Your driver's license, please.
Für wie lange?	For how long?

Getting gas

30 liters of (super/unleaded), please.	**Dreißig Liter (Super/bleifrei), bitte.**
self-service	**selbsttanken**
Fill it up, please.	**Einmal volltanken, bitte.**
I need some (air/water/oil), please.	**Ich brauche (Luft/Wasser/Öl), bitte.**

Checking the way

Is this the way to Berlin?	**Ist das der Weg nach Berlin?**
How far is Hamburg?	**Wie weit ist es nach Hamburg?**
Where is . . . ?	**Wo ist . . . ?**

(for numbers see Bare necessities p40)

Non-visual road and parking signs

freies Parken	free parking
Parkgebühr	fee for parking
rechts halten	keep right
Vorfahrt	right-of-way
Rastplatz	rest area
Gebühr	toll
Umleitung	detour
Abbiegung	turn off
Sackgasse	cul-de-sac
Einbahnstraße	one way
Abfahrt/Auffahrt	exit/approach to the highway

Using the subway

Does this train go to the main station? — **Fährt dieser Zug zum Haupt-bahnhof?**

Which (train/line) goes to town hall square? — **(Welcher Zug/Welche Linie) fährt zum Rathausplatz?**

Nehmen Sie die U1. — Take the U1 line.

Steigen Sie in . . . um. — Change at . . .

Buying a ticket

Where is the ticket office, please? — **Wo ist der Schalter bitte?**

A (single/round-trip) ticket, please. — **(Einfach/hin und zurück), bitte.**

a round-trip ticket — **eine Rückfahrkarte**

a daily travel card — **eine Tageskarte**

for two adults, one child — **zwei Erwachsene, ein Kind**

(1st/2nd) class — **(erster/zweiter) Klasse**

I'd like to reserve a (seat/berth), please. — **Ich möchte einen (Platz/Platz im Schlafwagen) reservieren, bitte.**

Raucher oder Nichtraucher? — Smoking or non-smoking?

Das kostet . . . Zuschlag. — There is a charge of . . .

Getting information on trains and buses

Are there (buses/trains) to . . . ? — **Gibt es (Busse/Züge) nach . . . ?**

From where does the train to Köln leave? — **Von wo fährt der Zug nach Köln?**

platform 8 — **Gleis acht/Bahnsteig acht**

When does the train depart? — **Wann fährt der Zug ab?**

When does the train arrive? — **Wann kommt der Zug an?**

When does the next train leave? — **Wann geht der nächste Zug?**

How long does the journey take? — **Wie lange dauert die Fahrt?**

Have you got a schedule? — **Haben Sie einen Fahrplan?**

Does this bus go to . . . ? — **Fährt dieser Bus nach . . . ?**

Can you tell me where to get off? — **Können Sie mir sagen, wo ich aussteigen muß?**

Steigen Sie in . . . aus. — Get off at . . .

Steigen Sie in . . . um. — Change at . . .

Ich zeige es Ihnen. — I'll show you.

Vehicles

das Flugzeug	plane
das Taxi	taxi
die Straßen-bahn	streetcar
die U-Bahn	subway

das Auto	car
der Zug	train
das Fahrrad	bike
der Bus	bus

Taking a taxi

Is there a taxi stand near here?	**Gibt es einen Taxistand in der Nähe?**
To this address, please.	**Zu dieser Adresse, bitte.**
How long is it?	**Wie lange dauert es?**
How far is it?	**Wie weit ist es?**
How much is it/will it be?	**Wieviel kostet es?**
Keep the change.	**Stimmt so.**
This is for you.	**Das ist für Sie.**
Can I have a receipt?	**Kann ich bitte eine Quittung haben?**
Nicht weit/lang.	Not far/long.

Signs

Abfahrt	departures	**Schlafwagen**	sleeping car
Ankunft	arrivals	**Auskunft/Information**	information
Bahnsteig/Gleis	platform	**Fahrstuhl**	elevator
Schalter	counter		
Wartesaal	waiting room		

Sound Check

Bahnhof: the "h" after a vowel makes the sound long
Apotheke, Kathedrale: the "h" after a "t" doesn't sound at all

Language works

Asking for things

1 Finding the way
- **Entschuldigung, wo ist das Museum, bitte?**
- □ **Das Museum? Das ist die nächste Straße links.**
- **Wie weit ist das, bitte?**
- □ **Ungefähr 500 Meter.**
- **Vielen Dank.**

(**ungefähr** = about)

Is the museum on the left or on the right?

2 Asking for the bus
- **Gibt es hier eine Bushaltestelle?**
- □ **Hier um die Ecke.**
- **Fährt der Bus in die Innenstadt?**
- □ **Ja, die Nummer neun.**

Is the bus stop far?
What bus goes to the center?

Renting things

3 Renting a car
- **Ich möchte bitte ein Auto mieten.**
- □ **Selbstverständlich. Was für ein Auto?**
- **Einen VW Golf, bitte. Was kostet das pro Woche?**
- □ **Das kostet 550 Mark pro Woche. Haben Sie Ihren Führerschein da?**
- **Natürlich, hier bitte.**

(**selbstverständlich/natürlich** = of course)

What type of car are we talking about?
How long can you have the car for, if you pay 550 marks?

4 How about a bike?
- **Wir möchten bitte zwei Fahrräder leihen.**
- □ **Das kostet zwölf Mark pro Tag, oder sechzig Mark pro Woche.**

How much do you save if you hire a bike for a week?

Traveling by car

5 Getting gas
- **Guten Tag, zwanzig Liter Super, bitte.**
- □ **Hier ist selbsttanken.**

What do you have to do?

6 What kind of gas
- **Einmal volltanken, bitte.**
- □ **Super oder bleifrei?**
- **Super, bitte.**

What do you need?
What are the options?

7 How to get to the autobahn.
- **Ich suche die Autobahn.**
- □ **Sie fahren hier die erste Straße rechts, dann geradeaus.**
- **Wie weit ist es nach Hannover?**

□ **Ungefähr einhundert Kilometer.**

Do you have to take the first or
second street on the right?
How far is it to Hannover?

Using transportation

8 Using the subway
■ **Entschuldigung, fährt dieser Zug
zum Hauptbahnhof?**
□ **Nein, nehmen Sie die U1.**

Are you on the right train?

9 A ticket to Munich
■ **Was kostet eine Rückfahrkarte
nach München, bitte?**
□ **Dreiundachtzig Mark. Möchten
Sie einen Platz reservieren?**
■ **Ja, bitte.**
□ **Das macht dann siebenund-
achtzig Mark.**

Is the price for a one-way or round-trip
ticket? What's the total?

10 Inquiring about the schedule
and platform
■ **Wann fährt der Zug nach
München ab?**
□ **Um acht Uhr siebzehn.**
■ **Und wann kommt er in München
an?**
□ **Um zehn Uhr drei.**
■ **Von wo fährt der Zug ab?**
□ **Gleis vierzehn.**

The train leaves at . . . from . . . and
arrives at . . . on . . .

(for time reference see p39)

Try it out

Puzzle

Can you guess the missing
words?

A
■ **Entschuldigung. Was kostet eine
Fahrkarte nach Köln?**
□ **Einfach kostet 37 Mark, hin und
. . . kostet 74 Mark.**
■ **Ich möchte einen . . . reservieren.
Und von wo fährt der Zug?**
□ **Von . . . dreizehn.**

B
■ **. . . ist die Bushaltestelle, bitte?**
□ **Hier . . . aus. Ungefähr zweihundert Meter.**

As if you were there

Finding the right words in
German

■ (Where is the tourist office,
please?)
□ **Sie gehen hier rechts und dann
die zweite links.**
■ (Is it far?)
□ **Nein, ungefähr zehn Minuten von
hier.**
■ (And is there a bank near
here?)
□ **Ja, in der Goethestraße. Die
zweite Straße links.**

Somewhere to stay

Germany has some of the world's most luxurious and expensive hotels, but in country regions you can sleep beneath downy featherbeds and breakfast on hearty farm fare for less than the cost of a meal in an average city restaurant. In between is an enormous range of moderately priced hotels and smaller family-run *Pensionen*. This is Germany, so of one thing you can be sure – all of them, whatever the room rate, offer clean and comfortable accommodation and efficient management.

Hotels

All the major international chains are represented in Germany, where some groups have also established flagship establishments, notably the two Kempinski hotels in Hamburg and Munich. There are specialist groups, like Silence, which guarantee that their hotels are located in quiet surroundings. The Gast im Schloß group has an impressive collection of castle hotels, while the Romantik group offers just what the name implies: romantic buildings, rooms and surroundings. All of the major group hotels (Hilton, Marriott, Sheraton, for example) have central booking arrangements, allowing you to reserve rooms from

abroad at no extra cost. A very useful central booking office is operated (free of charge) by ADZ, Corneliusstraße 34, 60325 Frankfurt/Main, tel. 069/740767, fax 069/751056.

Check before booking any city hotel whether there's a trade show during the time you plan to visit; not only will it be more difficult to find accommodations but room rates soar, sometimes as much as 50%. Most large hotels offer special weekend rates, but even if you're planning a weekday stay it always pays to ask whether special rates apply. Many hotels make no charge for children sharing their parents' room, and most if not all are willing to install an extra bed or cot at little or no cost. Most major hotels have special rooms or even floors for non-smokers and some have floors reserved for women.

Pensionen, Gasthäuser, Gasthöfe

Germany has no centrally directed star system for its hotels and other accommodations, although individual states are gradually introducing their own. Thus it is difficult for the visitor to judge the difference in comfort and facilities that can be expected in a hotel as opposed to a *Pension*. And the differences between a *Pension* and a typical German *Gasthaus* or *Gasthof* can be even more blurred. Usually, price is the best indicator.

Have you got a room?
Haben Sie ein Zimmer frei?

Pensionen are small, often privately run hotels offering bed and breakfast, but sometimes lacking a dining room for midday and evening meals. In that case, they usually describe themselves as *Garni*. Many small *Pensionen* are delightful stopovers, offering far superior accommodation to the usual run of hotels. Most of these insider-tips are family run and have a personal touch lacking in many hotels.

Gasthäuser (singular *Gasthaus*) and *Gasthöfe* (singular *Gasthof*) are more down-to-earth establishments, often village inns with their own wine or beer *Stube* (tavern) and restaurant. They offer good (and sometimes) extraordinary value for money.

Many private homes and farms in country regions offer bed and breakfast. Those that do usually hang up a sign advertising *Fremdenzimmer* (guest rooms). If they have vacancies, the sign will usually be accompanied by a green board reading *Zimmer frei* (vacancies). A red board reading *Belegt* means there are no vacancies. Local tourist offices have full lists of bed and breakfast possibilities.

Apartments and medium-term rentals

All tourist offices have lists of furnished apartments to let, and families on a fixed vacation budget should consider this option. Most major cities now have offices called *Wohnbörse* where furnished houses and apartments are offered for short- and medium-term rentals.

Farm vacations

The German Agricultural Association (DLG) produces a booklet listing more than 1,500 inspected and graded farms offering what the Germans call *Urlaub auf dem Bauernhof* (farm vacations). It's available from the DLG Reisedienst, Agratour, Eschborner Landstraße 122, 60489 Frankfurt/Main, tel. 069/247880.

Campers

Campers or tents are catered for in Germany by about 2,000 officially-inspected sites of very high standard, many of them in areas of great scenic beauty. Site fees are low and include the use of a range of facilities, from hot showers to supermarkets and restaurants. A list of campsites is available from the DCC, or German Camping Club, Mandelstraße 28, 80802 Munich, tel. 089/380 1420.

❗ Have you got a site for a camper?
⬤ **Haben Sie einen Stellplatz für einen Wohnwagen?**

Phrasemaker

Places to stay

das Ferienappartement	rental apartment
das Gästezimmer	guest room/B+B
das Gasthaus	guest house
das Hotel	hotel
das Rasthof	motel
der Campingplatz	campsite
der Gasthof	guest house
die Jugendherberge	youth hostel
die Pension	boarding house

Finding a place

I'd like to book a room.	**Ich möchte ein Zimmer reservieren.**
Have you got a room?	**Haben Sie ein Zimmer frei?**
Have you got a (single/ double) room?	**Haben Sie ein (Einzelzimmer/ Doppelzimmer)?**
for . . . nights	**für . . . Nächte**
May I see the room, please?	**Könnte ich das Zimmer sehen?**
Do you have anything cheaper?	**Haben Sie etwas Billigeres?**
I'll take it.	**Ich nehme es.**
I'll let you know.	**Ich sage Ihnen Bescheid.**
When do I have to check out?	**Wann muß ich das Zimmer verlassen?**

Herzlich willkommen.	Welcome.
Tut mir leid.	I'm sorry.
Alle Zimmer sind besetzt.	We are full.
Für wie viele (Nächte/Personen)?	For how many (nights/people)?
Kinder bezahlen die Hälfte.	Children half price.
Hier ist (das Anmeldeformular/ der Zimmerschlüssel).	Here is the (registration form/ key).
Frühstück ist von 7.30 Uhr bis 9.00 Uhr.	Breakfast is from 7:30 to 9:00 am.
(Frühstück/Mehrwertsteuer) ist nicht inklusive.	(Breakfast/tax) is not included.
Wählen Sie Null!	Dial zero.

Specifications

Does the room have a (shower/bath/phone/TV/child's bed)?	**Hat das Zimmer (eine Dusche/ein Bad/ein Telefon/einen Fernseher/ein Kinderbett)?**
How do I get an outside number?	**Wie telefoniere ich raus?**
Is there a (parking lot for guests/dining room/bar/elevator)?	**Gibt es (einen Parkplatz für Gäste/einen Speisesaal/eine Bar/einen Fahrstuhl)?**
Is breakfast included?	**Ist Frühstück inklusive?**
What time is breakfast?	**Wann gibt es Frühstück?**
Selbstverständlich./Nein, leider nicht.	Of course./Unfortunately not.
Ihren (Namen/Paß), bitte.	Your (name/passport), please.
Wie ist Ihre Autonummer?	What is your license plate number?

Checking in

I have a reservation for a room.	**Ich habe ein Zimmer bestellt.**
. . . in the name of . . .	**. . . auf den Namen . . .**

Problems

The (telephone/shower) is not working.	**(Das Telefon/Die Dusche) funktioniert nicht.**
How do you work the (shower/blind/heating)?	**Wie funktioniert (die Dusche/das Rollo/die Heizung)?**
There is no (soap/towel) in the room.	**Da ist (keine Seife/kein Handtuch) im Zimmer.**
Ich schicke jemanden.	I'll send someone.
Ich hole es Ihnen.	I'll get you some.

Asking for help

Could I have a wake-up call at . . .?	**Können Sie mich bitte um . . . telefonisch wecken?**
Have you got a safety deposit box?	**Haben Sie einen Safe?**
Do you have a map of the town?	**Haben Sie einen Stadtplan?**
Could you recommend a restaurant?	**Können Sie ein Restaurant empfehlen?**
Can you order me a taxi, please?	**Können Sie mir bitte ein Taxi bestellen?**

Checking out

I'd like to pay the bill.	**Ich möchte die Rechnung bezahlen.**
by (traveler's check/credit card)	**mit (Reisescheck/Kreditkarte)**
I'll pay cash.	**Ich zahle bar.**
I think there is a mistake.	**Ich glaube, da ist ein Fehler.**

Welche Zimmernummer?	What room number?
Wie möchten Sie zahlen?	How would you like to pay?
Unterschreiben Sie bitte hier.	Please sign here.

At the campsite

Have you got a site for (a tent/camper)?	**Haben Sie einen Stellplatz (für ein Zelt/für einen Wohnwagen)?**
We are two adults and three children.	**Wir sind zwei Erwachsene und drei Kinder.**
Where are the (showers/trash cans/restrooms)?	**Wo sind (die Duschen/die Mülleimer/die Toiletten)?**
Is there a (laundry/shop)?	**Gibt es (einen Waschsalon/ein Geschäft)?**

Wie lange bleiben Sie?	How long are you going to stay?
Schönen Aufenthalt!	Have a nice stay!
Das macht . . . pro Tag für (das Auto/das Zelt/den Wohnwagen).	That's . . . per day for (the car/tent/camper).

Café
Restaurant
Biergarten

Waldhäuschen

Fremdenzimmer

►►►

At the youth hostel

I'd like a bed for two nights. | **Ich möchte ein Bett für zwei Nächte.**

| **Haben Sie einen Jugendherbergs- ausweis?** | Have you got a membership card? |
| **Ihr Zimmer ist im (ersten/ zweiten/dritten) Stock.** | Your room is on the (1st/ 2nd/ 3rd) floor. |

Signs to look out for

Bügeleisen	iron	**Minibar**	minibar
Fahrstuhl	elevator	**Satelitenfern-**	satellite TV
Fernsehen	TV	**sehen**	
Heizung	heating	**Telefon**	phone
Kabelfernsehen	cable TV	**Zimmerservice**	room service
Klimaanlage	air-conditioning		

Things in a room that could go wrong

die Dusche	shower	**das Licht**	light
das Fenster	window	**das Rollo**	blind
die Fenster-	shutters	**das Schloß**	lock
läden		**die Steckdose**	socket
die Fern-	remote	**das Telefon**	phone
bedienung	control	**der Wasser-**	faucet
die Glühbirne	bulb	**hahn**	
die Heizung	heating		

JUGEND- GÄSTEHAUS Haager Weg 42

Services

die Bar	bar	**das Restaurant**	restaurant
der Fitneßraum	fitness center	**die Sauna**	sauna
der Garten	garden	**das Schwimm-**	pool
der Golfplatz	golf course	**bad**	
der Konferenz-	conference	**der Tennisplatz**	tennis court
raum	room	**die Terrasse**	terrace

Words you may have to recognize

Ausgang	exit	**Parken**	parking
Außer Betrieb	out of order	**verboten**	prohibited
bitte klingeln	ring the bell	**Rauchen**	smoking
drücken	push	**verboten**	prohibited
Eingang	entrance	**Vollpension**	all daily meals
Halbpension	one main meal		included
	included	**ziehen**	pull
Notausgang	emergency exit		

Jugendherberge: the "j" sounds like the English "y"

Language works

At the hotel

1 A room for a week
■ **Guten Tag. Ich möchte bitte ein Zimmer reservieren.**
□ **Selbstverständlich. Für wie viele Nächte?**
■ **Für eine Woche bitte.**
□ **Gut. Wie ist Ihr Name?**
■ **Heinrich Ganz.**
□ **Möchten Sie ein Einzelzimmer?**
■ **Nein, ein Doppelzimmer, bitte. Was kostet das?**
□ **Das sind sechshundertzwanzig Mark.**
■ **Nehmen Sie Kreditkarten?**
□ **Natürlich.**

What information do you have to give? How much is the room?

2 Checking in
■ **Herzlich willkommen. Sie möchten ein Zimmer?**
□ **Ja, bitte. Ein Einzelzimmer für eine Nacht.**
■ **Das ist kein Problem. Hier ist das Anmeldeformular. Bitte unterschreiben Sie hier.**

You get a registration form. What do you have to do with it?

3 At a hotel
■ **Wann muß ich das Zimmer verlassen?**
□ **Um zehn Uhr. Frühstück ist von sieben Uhr bis neun Uhr.**

When do you have to check out? Until when is breakfast served?

■ **Entschuldigung. Haben Sie ein Zimmer frei?**
□ **Tut mir leid. Alle Zimmer sind besetzt.**

Can you stay at this hotel?

4 Using the services
■ **Hier ist Ihr Zimmerschlüssel. Das Zimmer ist im ersten Stock.**
□ **Hat das Zimmer einen Fernseher?**
■ **Nein, leider nicht.**

(see p46 for directions)

Where is your room?
Does it have a TV?

■ **Sagen Sie, gibt es einen Parkplatz für Gäste?**
□ **Selbstverständlich. Aber leider sind alle Plätze besetzt.**

Will you be able to leave your car in the hotel parking lot?

■ **Wann ist Frühstück, bitte?**
□ **Von sieben Uhr bis acht Uhr dreißig.**
■ **Können Sie mich bitte wecken?**
□ **Gern. Wann denn?**
■ **Um sieben Uhr dreißig.**
(**gern** = with pleasure)

What service is available?

■ **Nehmen Sie Kreditkarten, oder Schecks?**
□ **Kreditkarten ja, aber keine Schecks.**

How can you pay?

A place to stay

5 At the campsite
- Guten Tag. Haben Sie einen Stellplatz für einen Wohnwagen?
- ☐ Ja, sicher. Wie viele Personen sind Sie?
- Wir sind zwei Erwachsene und zwei Kinder.
- ☐ Wie lange bleiben Sie?
- Drei Wochen, bitte.

Camper or tent?
How many people in total?

- Gut. Hier ist das Anmeldeformular. Die Duschen und Toiletten sind hier links. Schönen Aufenthalt.
- ☐ Danke.

What facilities are there?
Where do you find them?

6 At the youth hostel
- Ich möchte ein Bett für eine Woche.
- ☐ Haben sie einen Jugendherbergsausweis?
- Ja, bitte.
- ☐ Gut. Ihr Zimmer ist im dritten Stock, Nummer dreihunderteins.

What do you need to stay here?
Where's your room?

Try it out

Puzzle

Unscramble the words
1 noWawnheg
2 apSiesaesl
3 zarkPptal
4 oiePnns
5 sssmmlleeZrhci
6 seeztBt
7 küühFtcsr
8 hesnrereF

Matching sentences

Does it make sense? Put the sentences in order.
- Für wie viele Nächte?
- ☐ Zwei Erwachsene.
- Hat das Zimmer Telefon?
- ☐ Im Speisesaal.
- Wo gibt es Frühstück?
- ☐ Alle Zimmer sind besetzt.
- Wie viele Personen sind Sie?
- ☐ Eine Woche, bitte.
- Haben Sie Zimmer frei?
- ☐ Nein, aber einen Fernseher.

As if you were there

Find the words in German
- Herzlich willkommen. Möchten Sie ein Zimmer?
- ☐ (You would like a double and a single room)
- Selbstverständlich. Für wie viele Nächte?
- ☐ (For four nights, please. Ask if the double room has a phone)
- Ja, natürlich. Möchten Sie das Zimmer mit Dusche oder Bad?
- ☐ (Say that you'd like a shower)

Buying things

Whether it's Meißen china, a Black Forest cuckoo clock or Munich beer steins, the range and quality of German goods vying for a visitor's attention and pocket is so huge it can make shopping a frustrating experience. All supermarkets help out, however, by having special sections stocked with typical regional products likely to interest visitors.

Antiques

Antique shops in cities and larger towns tend to congregate in specific areas, making shopping easier. In Northern Germany, comb the antique shops of Hamburg, Bremen, Kiel and other coastal towns for nautical items at knockdown prices.

Department stores and shopping malls

The range of department stores in Germany is probably unequaled in Europe, from individual establishments like Berlin's KaDeWe (one of mainland Europe's biggest) to countrywide chains such as Kaufhof, Karstadt and Hertie. Shopping malls are particularly popular among Germans, especially during sub-zero winter months. Hamburg claims to have Europe's largest area of covered shopping malls, on one bank of the Binnenalster lake.

How much is this?
Was kostet das?

Arts and crafts

Every German region has its own tradition of locally produced crafts. Glass blowers are at work throughout the Bavarian Forest, where you can buy direct from the glassworks and even watch your ordered piece taking shape before your eyes. A long tradition of jewelry-making is undergoing a revival, and goldsmiths are establishing themselves everywhere. German pottery has a long and distinguished tradition, and a potter's wheel can be seen spinning in backstreet studios of many Bavarian and Black Forest communities. In Bavarian towns like Berchtesgaden and Oberammergau you'll find bearded woodcarvers as gnarled as the wood they're working on. Wooden toys are the speciality of Franconian and Thuringian craft workers, whose products fill the stalls of Germany's lovely Christmas markets.

Flea markets

Europe's biggest flea market has grown up on Munich's former airport, Riem. It takes place every Saturday and Sunday – like virtually all Germany's other flea markets (Berlin and Frankfurt compete with Munich for scale). Hamburg's Sunday fish market has extended over the years into a colourful jumble of stalls offering much more than just North Sea cod.

That's too expensive!
Das ist zu teuer!

Food markets

Every town has its weekly market.
Berlin has a permanent market in
every one of its constituent urban
areas, while Munich has two markets
of great charm: the Viktualienmarkt
and Elisabethmarkt. A market isn't
only a place where Germans shop;
they treat their markets as meeting
places, where gossip is exchanged
and where business deals are done
across the bare, scrubbed table of a
market beer stall. If you're looking
for somewhere to eat well and
cheaply, make for the nearest
market: the menu includes a juicy
slice of local life.

> A grilled sausage with a roll,
> please.
> **Eine Bratwurst mit Brötchen,
> bitte.**

Porcelain and ceramics

The royal porcelain manufacturers
of three great German dynasties are
still in business, producing articles of
historical beauty (at prices to match).
In Berlin, you can find at the former
royal Prussian porcelain factory (the
Königliche Porzellanmanufactur)
delicate, hand-painted china which
once graced the tables of German
kings and queens. In Munich,
Nymphenburg porcelain bears the
name of the summer palace of the
Wittelsbachs, where fine china is still
produced by traditional methods.
Meißen is now producing again for
an expanding export market.

Visitors can buy directly from the
factory on the outskirts of town. On
a more mundane level, go hunting
for a genuine German garden gnome
among the tribes which people the
factories and shops of Lauterbach,
on the picturesque *Märchenstraße*
("Fairy Tale Route"). Smaller fairy
tale figures crafted by Hummel can
be found in most larger stores and
porcelain boutiques. Further along
the Fairy Tale Route, Hameln
(Hamelin of "Pied Piper" renown)
turns out more rat replicas than the
original population of rodents the
Piper was engaged to eradicate.

> Do you take credit cards?
> **Nehmen Sie Kreditkarten?**

Shops and banks

Legislation liberalizing
Germany's outmoded
shopping hours took effect
in November 1996, finally
bringing the country into
line with most of the rest of
Europe. The controversial
law allows shops to open
between 7 am and 8 pm
on weekdays and 7 am
and 4 pm on Saturdays.

Although some German shop-
keepers will bargain over prices, it's
not to be recommended. Some do
however, offer a discount for cash.
Credit cards are accepted by all
department stores and most large
shops, although many smaller
establishments and boutiques
require cash, traveler's checks
or Eurocheques.

Banks open Monday to Friday
from 8:30 am or 9 am and close at
3 pm or 4 pm, with an hour's lunch
break. Airports and main railway
stations have bank branches which
open every day as early as 7 am and
close as late as 10:30 pm.

Phrasemaker

Phrases to use anywhere

Have you got any (stamps/cheese/jeans)?	**Haben Sie (Briefmarken/Käse/Jeans)?**
How much is it?	**Was kostet das?**
How much is the total?	**Was kostet das zusammen?**
Can I pay (with traveler's checks/by credit card)?	**Kann ich (mit Reiseschecks/Kreditkarte) bezahlen?**
How much is the (wine/chocolate)?	**Was kostet (der Wein/die Schokolade)?**
How much are the (CDs/postcards)?	**Was kosten die (CDs/Postkarten)?**
Where do I get cigarettes?	**Wo bekomme ich Zigaretten?**
A (magazine/CD), please.	**Eine (Zeitschrift/CD), bitte.**
Thanks, that's all.	**Danke, das ist alles.**

Was kann ich für Sie tun?	Can I help you?
Was hätten Sie gern?	What would you like?
Leider nicht.	Unfortunately not.
Bitte schön.	There you are.
Dort drüben.	Over there.
Sonst noch etwas?	Anything else?
Das macht . . .	That's . . . altogether.

Types of shops

bakery	**die Bäckerei**
butcher shop	**der Metzger/der Fleischer**
department store	**das Kaufhaus**
market	**der Markt**
newsstand	**der Zeitschriftenhändler**
pharmacy	**die Apotheke/die Drogerie**
post office	**die Post**
stand	**der Kiosk**
supermarket	**der Supermarkt**

At the newsstand

ballpoint pen	**der Kugelschreiber**	magazine	**die Zeitschrift**
camera film	**der Film**	map of town	**der Stadtplan**
chocolate	**die Schokolade**	newspaper	**die Zeitung**
cigarette	**die Zigarette**	notepaper	**das Briefpapier**
lighter	**das Feuerzeug**	postcard	**die Ansichtskarte**

Souvenirs

der Aufkleber	sticker	das Porzellan	porcelain
der Bierkrug	beer mug	das Poster	poster
die Birken-stockschuhe	birkenstocks	die Postkarte	postcard
		der Reiseführer	travel guide
das Buch	book	das Schiff in	ship in a
die CD	CD	der Flasche	bottle
die Kassette	cassette	der Schmuck	jewelry
die Kuckucks-uhr	cuckoo clock	die Schokolade	chocolate
		die Schwarz-waldpuppe	doll from Black Forest
der Kugel-schreiber	ballpoint pen	der Tiroler Hut	hat from Tyrol
die Kuhglocke	cow's bell	die Uhr	watch
der Matrosen-hut	sailor's hat	der Wander-stock	walking stick
		der Wein	wine

(for things to buy at a pharmacy see Emergencies p101)

Food shopping

How much is (it/a kilo)?	**Wieviel kostet (das/ein Kilo)?**
A kilo of apples, please.	**Ein Kilo Äpfel, bitte.**
half a kilo of grapes	**ein Pfund Trauben**
100 grams of ham	**100 Gramm Schinken**
a jar/packet of . . .	**ein Glas/eine Packung . . .**
a slice of salami	**eine Scheibe Salami**
Can I try (some/a piece)?	**Kann ich (etwas/ein Stück) probieren?**
A bit (more/less), please.	**Ein bißchen (mehr/weniger), bitte.**
I'll take three, please.	**Ich nehme drei Stück, bitte.**
I'd like a cheese roll, please.	**Ich möchte ein Käsebrötchen, bitte.**
Wieviel möchten Sie?	How much would you like?
Das macht . . . zusammen.	That's . . . in total.

Measurements and containers

das Glas	jar	die Dose	can
das Kilo	kilo	die Flasche	bottle
das Pfund	half a kilo	die Packung	packet
der Becher	cup/pot		

63

Fruit and vegetables

der Apfel	apple	die Melone	melon
die Banane	banana	die Orange	orange
die Birne	pear	der Pfirsich	peach
der Blumenkohl	cauliflower	die Pflaume	plum
die Bohne	bean	der Rosenkohl	Brussels sprouts
die Erbse	pea	der Rotkohl	red cabbage
die Erdbeere	strawberry	der Salat	lettuce
die Gurke	cucumber	die Tomate	tomato
die Karotte	carrot	die Traube	grape
die Kartoffel	potato	der Weißkohl	cabbage
die Kirsche	cherry	die Zitrone	lemon
die Kiwi	kiwi fruit	die Zwiebel	onion

Fish and meat

die Bratwurst	grilled sausage	die Makrele	mackerel
der Dorsch	cod	die Muschel	mussel
die Ente	duck	die Pute	turkey
der Fisch	fish	das Rindfleisch	beef
das Hähnchen	chicken	der Schinken	ham
der Heilbutt	halibut	die Scholle	sole
der Hering	herring	das Schweine-fleisch	pork
der Hummer	lobster	die Wurst	sausage
das Kotelett	pork chop		
das Lamm-fleisch	lamb		

Groceries

der Apfelsaft	apple juice	der Rasier-schaum	shaving cream
das Bier	beer	die Sahne	cream
die Butter	butter	der Sekt	sparkling wine
die Cola	cola	die Seife	soap
der Joghurt	yogurt	das Shampoo	shampoo
der Kaffee	coffee	das Taschen-tuch	tissue
der Käse	cheese	der Tee	tea
die Limonade	lemonade	das Toiletten-papier	toilet paper
die Margarine	margarine	der Wein	wine
die Milch	milk	die Zahnbürste	toothbrush
das Mineral-wasser	mineral water	die Zahnpasta	toothpaste
der Orangensaft	orange juice		
die Rasier-klinge	razor blade		

Bread, pastries and cakes

der Apfelstrudel	apple strudel
das Bauernbrot	bread made from a sourdough
der Berliner	doughnut
der Bienenstich	sticky pastry filled with sweet cream
die Brezel	pretzel
das Brot	bread
das Brötchen	bread roll
das Hörnchen	type of croissant
die Marzipantorte	marzipan cake
der Mohnkuchen	poppy seed cake
die Nußtorte	cream cake with nuts
der Pumpernickel	heavy dark bread
die Sachertorte	chocolate cake
das Schwarzbrot	dark bread
die Schwarzwälder Kirschtorte	Black Forest cake
der Streuselkuchen	crumble cake
das Vollkornbrot	heavy wheat bread
der Zwetschgenkuchen	type of plum cake

Delicatessen

das Beefsteackhack	raw minced beef eaten on bread
das Gerstenbier	beer made from barley
das Weißbier	wheat beer
der Aufschnitt	cold meat
der Edamer	Edam cheese
der Fleischsalat	sliced sausage/cold meat and gherkins in a mayonnaise dressing
der geräucherte Aal	smoked eel
der Heringssalat	pieces of herring with onion in sour cream
der Moselwein	wine from the Moselle
der Rheinwein	wine from the Rhine
das Schmalz	lard, eaten on bread
der Schwarzwälder Schinken	type of smoked ham
die Leberwurst	liver pâté
die Sülze	headcheese
die Teewurst	sausage spread

Buying clothes

I'm just looking, thank you.	**Ich schau nur, danke.**
Where do I find sweaters?	**Wo finde ich Pullover?**
Where is the (ladies'/mens'/ household) department?	**Wo ist die (Damen-, Herren-, Haushalts-) abteilung?**
Is there an elevator?	**Gibt es einen Fahrstuhl?**
I'd like a (shirt/pair of pants).	**Ich möchte (ein Hemd/eine Hose).**
I'm size (10/12/14).	**Ich habe Größe (38/40/42).**
Have you got size . . . ?	**Haben Sie Größe . . . ?**
Can I try it on?	**Kann ich es anprobieren?**
It's a bit (big/small).	**Es ist ein bißchen (groß/klein).**
Have you got this (bigger/ smaller/cheaper)?	**Haben Sie es (größer/kleiner/ billiger)?**
Do you have the same in yellow?	**Haben Sie das auch in Gelb?**
I like (it/them).	**Es gefällt mir/Sie gefallen mir.**
I don't like (it/them).	**Es gefällt mir nicht/Sie gefallen mir nicht.**
I'll take (it/them).	**Ich nehme (es/sie).**
I'll think about it.	**Ich überlege es mir.**
Do you take (credit cards/ checks)?	**Nehmen Sie (Kreditkarten/ Schecks)?**
Welche (Größe/Farbe)?	What (size/color)?
Das kann ich empfehlen.	I can recommend that.
im Erdgeschoß	on the first floor
im (ersten/zweiten/dritten) Stock	on the (2nd/3rd/4th) floor
im Untergeschoß	in the basement

Clothes

der Anzug	suit	**der Rock**	skirt
der Badeanzug	bathing suit	**der Schal**	scarf
die Badehose	trunks	**der Schuh**	shoe
der Bikini	bikini	**die Socke**	sock
die Bluse	blouse	**der Stiefel**	boot
der Gürtel	belt	**die Strickjacke**	cardigan
die Handschuhe	gloves	**der Strumpf**	stocking
das Hemd	shirt	**die Strumpfhose**	tights
die Hose	pants	**der Trainings- anzug**	sweat suit
der Hut	hat		
das Jackett	suit jacket	**das T-Shirt**	t-shirt
die Jeans	pair of jeans		
das Kleid	dress		
das Kostüm	suit (skirt+ jacket)		
die Krawatte	tie		
der Mantel	coat		
die Mütze	woolen hat		
der Pullover	sweater		
die Regenjacke	rain jacket		

Materials

die Wolle	wool	**die Seide**	silk
die Schurwolle	pure wool	**das Leder**	leather
die Baumwolle	cotton	**das Plastik**	plastic
das Nylon	nylon	**das Goretex**	goretex
die Angorawolle	angora	**das Frottee**	terry cloth

(For colors see Bare necessities p40)

At the post office

Excuse me, where do I have to wait?	**Entschuldigung, wo muß ich mich anstellen?**
How much is a (postcard/letter) to England?	**Was kostet (eine Postkarte/ein Brief) nach England?**
Two (50-Pfennig/one-mark) stamps, please.	**Zwei Briefmarken zu (fünfzig Pfennig/einer Mark), bitte.**
Two phone cards for 10 DM, please.	**Zwei Telefonkarten zu zehn Mark, bitte.**
I'd like to send this to Australia.	**Ich möchte das nach Australien schicken.**

Schalter sechs.	Window six.
Luft- oder Landweg?	By airmail or ground mail?

Getting photographic equipment

A film for (prints/slides).	**Einen Film für (Fotos/Dias).**
I'd like some batteries, please.	**Ich hätte gern Batterien.**
Can you develop this?	**Können Sie das entwickeln lassen?**
When can I pick it up?	**Wann kann ich es abholen?**

Vierundzwanzig oder sechsunddreißig Bilder?	24 or 36 exposures?
Heute/Morgen/in einer Stunde/in zwei Stunden.	Today/tomorrow/in an hour/in two hours.

Sound Check

Käse: the **ä** sounds like "ay" in English "day" but long
Briefmarken: the **ie** is a long "ee" sound

Language works

Buying things

1 Buying a souvenir
■ **Was kann ich für Sie tun?**
□ **Haben Sie Aufkleber von Stuttgart?**
■ **Ja, hier sind welche für zwei Mark.**
□ **Haben Sie auch Reiseführer?**
■ **Dort drüben.**
□ **Ich nehme zwei Aufkleber und diesen Reiseführer.**
■ **Das macht siebzehn Mark achtzig, bitte.**

If the stickers are two marks each, can you figure out how much the travel guide is?

2 Trying some German bread or cake
■ **Guten Tag, was bekommen Sie?**
□ **Sechs Brötchen und zwei Stück Kuchen.**
■ **Sonst noch etwas?**
□ **Ja, bitte. Haben Sie Bauernbrot?**
■ **Leider nicht, aber Vollkornbrot.**
□ **Gut, das nehme ich.**

Instead of the Bauernbrot, you are offered bread rolls/wheat bread/dark bread.

3 At the counter in the supermarket
■ **Was hätten Sie gern?**
□ **Ich möchte Aufschnitt, bitte.**

■ **Schinken? Salami? Teewurst?**
□ **Bitte zweihundert Gramm Schinken. Und haben Sie Leberwurst?**
■ **Tut mir leid. Die bekommen Sie nur im Glas.**

Do you get the pâté in a jar or a can?

Shopping at the department store

4 Where is it?
■ **Entschuldigung, wo finde ich die Damenabteilung?**
■ **Dritter Stock, rechts.**
■ **Gibt es einen Fahrstuhl?**
□ **Ja, dort drüben.**

When you get to the third floor, do you go right, left or straight on?

5 Buying clothes
■ **Ich möchte eine Hose.**
□ **Welche Größe?**
■ **Größe 40. Haben Sie die auch in Blau?**
□ **Ja, hier. Bitte schön.**
■ **Gut. Ich nehme die Hose, die Bluse und das Hemd.**
□ **Also, die Hose kostet vierundachtzig Mark, die Bluse dreiundvierzig und das Hemd zweiundvierzig Mark.**

Which item was the most expensive and which the cheapest one?

Postcards and photos

6 At the post office
- **Guten Tag. Was kostet eine Karte nach England?**
- □ **Achtzig Pfennig.**
- **Drei Briefmarken zu achtzig Pfennig und eine Telefonkarte zu zwanzig Mark.**

How much is a stamp for England: 0.50, 0.80, 1.20?
What's the total?

7 Getting film developed
- **Ich habe einen Film. Können Sie den entwickeln lassen?**
- □ **Selbstverständlich.**
- **Wann kann ich ihn abholen?**
- □ **In einer Stunde.**

How long do you have to wait for your prints?
Do you have to stay another day?

Try it out

As if you were there

At the newsstand
- (Ask how much the ballpoint pen is.)
- □ **Eine Mark zwanzig das Stück.**
- (Ask if they have English magazines.)
- □ **Nein, tut mir leid. Nur Zeitungen.**
- (Say that you would like two postcards.)
- □ **Das macht zwei Mark.**
- (Say thank you and goodbye.)

Sending some cards home
- (Ask where you have to wait.)
- □ **Dort drüben. Schalter drei.**
- (Ask how much a letter to Australia is.)
- □ **Eine Mark achtzig.**

Adding up

two chocolate bars
eine Mark zwanzig
an English newspaper
drei Mark fünfzehn
two postcards
zwei Mark
Das kostet zusammen: . . . DM

Word game

The first letters of the following words give a new word:

The word for "ten"

_ _ _ _
What do you say to get attention?

_ _ _ _ _ _ _ _ _ _ _ _ _ _
. . . möchte drei Bananen

_ _ _
The word for "grape"

_ _ _ _ _ _
The word for "and"

_ _ _
. . . Sie Kreditkarten?

_ _ _ _ _ _
Haben Sie . . . 40?

_ _ _ _ _

Café life

Café life

Germans love their coffee and cakes and you will find plenty of cafés to try *Kaffee und Kuchen* yourself. German tea-time means coffee and great wedges of cake, although most Germans are too busy to take enough time off on weekdays for what has long become a weekend ritual. Black Forest cake and Viennese Sachertorte have taken over in cafés everywhere. An afternoon invitation to a German home invariably means unlimited coffee accompanied by at least two freshly baked cakes.

> ❗ I'd like a piece of Black Forest cake and a cup of coffee, please.
> **Ich möchte ein Stück Schwarzwälder Kirschtorte und eine Tasse Kaffee, bitte.**

Types of cafés

You will discover many different types of cafés in Germany. They range from the Viennese coffeehouse style to a small café attached to a bakery or a café in a department store. To find your favorite café it is best to have a look at the inside as well as the menu.

Most cafés serve a wide variety of cakes as well as light savory snacks. And don't miss the delicious ice cream served in most cafés! Especially when many cafés serve their delicious coffee, cakes and ice creams outside as soon as temperatures rise.

Phrasemaker
In the café

I'd like a piece of (apple /fruit/ Black Forest/chocolate/ cream) cake.

Ich möchte ein Stück (Apfel-kuchen/Obstkuchen/ Schwarzwälder Kirschtorte/ Schokoladentorte/Sahnetorte).

Have you got any (strawberry ice cream/cherry ice cream/ hot chocolate)?

Haben Sie (Erdbeereis/Kirscheis/ heiße Schokolade)?

What soft drinks do you have?

Welche alkoholfreien Getränke haben Sie?

I'll have (coffee/tea), please.

Ich nehme (Kaffee/Tee), bitte.

This one, please.

Diesen hier, bitte.

Do you serve outside?

Bedienen Sie draußen?

Was möchten Sie, bitte?
What would you like?

Tut mir leid, wir haben kein . . . mehr.
Sorry, we've run out of . . .

Kommt sofort!
Won't be a minute!

Was trinken Sie?
What would you like to drink?

Kännchen oder Tasse?
A small pot or a cup?

Ja, einen Moment.
Yes, just a minute.

Mit (Eis/Zitrone/Sahne)?
With (ice/lemon/cream)?

Mit Kohlensäure oder ohne Kohlensäure?
Sparkling or still?

Welchen?
Which one?

Welchen Geschmack?
What flavor?

Bitte zahlen Sie an der Kasse.
Please pay at the register.

Other helpful phrases

Where are the restrooms, please?
Wo sind die Toiletten, bitte?

Is there a telephone?
Gibt es hier ein Telefon?

How much is it?
Was kostet das?

Here you are.
Bitte schön.

Please refer to p77 in the Eating out section for a comprehensive list of foods to order

Containers

der Becher mug
die Dose can
die Flasche bottle
das Glas glass
das Kännchen pot

die Karaffe jug
die Portion portion
das Stück piece/slice
die Tasse cup
der Teller plate

Sound Check

möchte: the "**ch**" is a soft sound as in "loch"

draußen: "**ß**" is a sharp sound as in double "s"

Language works

In a café

1 Ordering cake
- **Haben Sie Obstkuchen?**
- ☐ **Ja, Apfelkuchen. Und was trinken Sie?**
- **Eine Tasse heiße Schokolade, bitte.**
- ☐ **Kommt sofort!**

What type of fruit cake are you offered?

2 Ordering coffee gives you a choice
- **Ich nehme Kaffee, bitte.**
- ☐ **Kännchen oder Tasse?**

What are the options?

3 Sitting outside
- **Bedienen Sie draußen?**
- ☐ **Ja, einen Moment.**
  Was bekommen Sie?
- **Ein Stück Schwarzwälder Kirschtorte.**

- ☐ **Tut mir leid. Das haben wir nicht. Möchten Sie Schokoladentorte?**
- **Nein, danke.**

Are you offered chocolate ice cream, Black Forest cake or chocolate cake?

Try it out

Dialogue

This dialogue set in a café is jumbled up. Can you find the correct order of these phrases?

- **Eine Tasse, bitte.**
- ☐ **Selbstverständlich. Und was trinken Sie?**
- **Ein Stück Apfelkuchen, bitte.**
- ☐ **Kommt sofort.**
- **Kaffee, bitte.**
- ☐ **Guten Tag, was bekommen Sie?**
- ☐ **Kännchen oder Tasse?**

Missing words

A few words are missing in this dialogue. Can you fill the blanks?

- Haben Sie Obstkuchen?
- □ Ja, die Schokoladentorte ist gut.
- □ Mit Zitrone?
- □ Ja, Apfelkuchen.

- Ich nehme Kaffee, bitte.
- □ Das macht 3,50 DM, bitte.
- □ Mit oder ohne Kohlensäure?
- □ Und was trinken Sie?

- Welche alkoholfreien Getränke haben Sie?
- □ Wir haben Bier und Limonade.
- □ Mineralwasser, Limonade, Cola, ...
- □ Erdbeereis, Schokoladentorte.

Which one is it?

Find the odd one out!

- Haben . . . . . Schokoladentorte?
- □ Tut mir . . . . . Schokoladentorte haben wir nicht, aber Schwarzwälder Kirschtorte.
- Gut, dann Schwarzwälderkirsch. Und eine . . . . . Kaffee.
- □ Kaffee haben wir nur im . . . . .
- Dann nehme ich Mineral . . . . .
- □ Kommt . . . . .

Which answer matches?

Find the matching response for each section.

- Ich möchte Mineralwasser.
- □ Welchen Geschmack?
- □ Mit Kohlensäure?
- □ Kännchen oder Tasse?

A Schokolade, Kaffee, Tee, Mineralwasser.

B Apfelkuchen, Kirscheis, Obstkuchen, Erdbeertorte.

C Kännchen, Tasse, Sahne, Becher.

D Tut mir leid, Kommt sofort, Was bekommen Sie?, Einen Moment, bitte.

E ein Stück, eine Tasse, ein Becher, ein Kännchen.

Eating out

Germans love to eat out, and some city restaurants are so busy that they never close. In Berlin, Hamburg and Munich there are many popular places to eat where you can talk the night away after supper, stay for breakfast and continue on until lunch.

Breakfasting German-style

For a country which has embraced the so-called continental breakfast of coffee and rolls, there is still a strong tradition of hearty breakfast eating, which is catered for handsomely by an increasing number of cafés and early-opening bars. In Hamburg, all-night revellers are encouraged to breakfast on freshly-caught fish at quayside bars and restaurants, while in Bavaria many firms allow a breakfast break for workers who tuck into *Weißwurst* (the local white sausage), *Leberkäs* (a kind of meat loaf) and pretzels. Indeed, tradition demands that *Weißwurst* should not be eaten after midday, so it's distinctly a breakfast dish.

Light lunches

Lunch breaks are consequently short, and so are lunchtime menus.

Evening dining

Evening meals are served relatively early in German restaurants, from about 7 pm on, but kitchens generally stay open until midnight or later.

**❗ A table for two people, please.
Einen Tisch für zwei Personen,
◗ bitte.**

The German routine

Visitors to Germany are well advised to choose a hotel offering a buffet-style breakfast and to have lunch German-style: in the city, at a marketplace stall or at any of the German, Greek or Turkish deli-catessens which line central streets; in the country, at a simple inn (if there's a *Gasthof zur Post* go there; the food and the beer are invariably good). A typical restaurant or tavern menu will have soup as an appetizer (German soups are deservedly famous) and a meat-based dish (usually pork or veal) as a main course. Germans have long since acquired a taste for Italian pasta and pizza, and Italian restaurants are everywhere (Munich can compete with many Italian cities for the number and quality of its Italian restaurants).

Children

Restaurants, taverns and even bars place no restrictions on the admission of children, and many cater to young guests with special menus. Fast-food chains have penetrated every corner of Germany, and while the quality of their food may be debatable, they offer excellent value for families.

And the not-so-young

In most resorts and spas specially-priced *Seniorenteller* (literally "dishes for senior citizens"!) can be requested by elderly visitors.

Vegetarians

Germany is historically a big meat-eating nation, and vegetarians had a lean time until recently. But vegetarian cuisine is increasingly taking hold, and most restaurants now have a choice of vegetarian dishes, albeit often very limited. A big surprise is that Munich's temple of roast pork, dumplings and copious beer, the *Hofbräuhaus*, serves up some of the city's most imaginative vegetarian specialities. All major cities and most large towns have exclusively vegetarian restaurants, and they are listed in tourist office guides.

❗ Do you have vegetarian dishes?
⬤ **Haben Sie vegetarische Gerichte?**

Phrasemaker

Signs of places

der Biergarten	beer garden	**der Imbiß**	snack bar
das Café	café	**die Kneipe**	pub
die Eisdiele	ice-cream parlor	**die Konditorei**	café

At the restaurant

ashtray	**der Aschenbecher**	pepper	**der Pfeffer**
bottle	**die Flasche**	plate	**der Teller**
bowl (dessert)	**die Schale**	salt	**das Salz**
bowl (soup)	**der Suppenteller**	saucer	**die Untertasse**
chair	**der Stuhl**	spoon	**der Löffel**
cup	**die Tasse**	table	**der Tisch**
fork	**die Gabel**	tablecloth	**die Tischdecke**
glass	**das Glas**	teaspoon	**der Teelöffel**
knife	**das Messer**	toothpick	**der Zahnstocher**
napkin	**die Serviette**	vinegar	**der Essig**
oil	**das Öl**		

Arriving

A table for (one/two) people, please.	**Einen Tisch für (eine Person/zwei Personen), bitte.**
We have a reservation for three.	**Wir haben eine Reservierung für drei Personen.**
I'd like to reserve a table.	**Ich möchte einen Tisch reservieren.**
Is this table free?	**Ist dieser Tisch noch frei?**
Excuse me, is this self-service?	**Entschuldigung, ist hier Selbstbedienung?**
Where (is/are) the (trays/cutlery/glasses), please?	**Wo (ist/sind) (die Tabletts/das Besteck/die Gläser), bitte?**

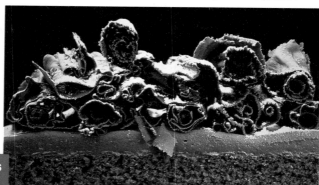

Asking about the menu

The menu, please.	**Die Speisekarte, bitte.**
What is the special today?	**Was ist das Tagesgericht?**
What is . . .?	**Was ist . . .?**
Can you recommend anything?	**Können Sie etwas empfehlen?**
Have you got . . .?	**Haben Sie . . .?**
Is the tip included?	**Ist das mit Bedienung?**

Ordering

I'd like to order.	**Ich möchte bestellen.**
I'd like (a grilled sausage with french fries/a pork chop with salad/ a slice of pizza).	**Ich möchte (eine Bratwurst mit Pommes frites/ein Kotelett mit Salat/ein Stück Pizza).**
a (curry/cooked) sausage	**eine Currywurst/Bockwurst**
a (kebab/ham sausage)	**ein Schaschlik/Schinkenwurst**
I'd like the . . .	**Ich möchte/nehme . . .**
chicken with rice	**das Hähnchen mit Reis**
roast beef with potatoes and vegetables	**den Rinderbraten mit Kartoffeln und Gemüse**
I'll have . . . as an (appetizer/ main course/side dish/ dessert).	**Ich nehme . . . als (Vorspeise/ Hauptspeise/Beilage/ Nachtisch).**
No dessert, thank you.	**Keinen Nachtisch, danke.**
I'll have (a glass/a bottle) of (white wine/red wine/beer/ mineral water).	**Ich trinke (ein Glas/eine Flasche) (Weißwein/Rotwein/Bier/ Mineralwasser).**
Do you have (sandwiches/ vegetarian dishes)?	**Haben Sie (belegte Brote/ vegetarische Gerichte)?**

Haben Sie schon gewählt?	Have you decided?
Was bekommen Sie?	What would you like?
Heute haben wir . . .	Today we have . . .
Wie möchten Sie das?	How would you like it?
Tut mir leid, wir haben kein . . .	Sorry, we don't have any . . .
Es ist (Fisch/ein Gemüse/ eine Soße).	It's (fish/a vegetable/a sauce).
Besteck ist dort drüben.	The cutlery is over there.
Guten Appetit!	Enjoy your meal!

Ordering drinks

a bottle/half a bottle of red/white/rosé wine	**eine Flasche/eine halbe Flasche Rotwein/Weißwein/Roséwein**
a beer	**ein Bier**
a (still/sparkling) mineral water	**ein Mineralwasser (ohne Kohlensäure/mit Kohlensäure)**

Eating habits

I'm allergic to . . .	**Ich bin gegen . . . allergisch.**
I'm vegetarian.	**Ich bin Vegetarier.**
Does it contain . . . ?	**Ist das mit . . . ?**

During the meal

Excuse me! Waiter!/Waitress!	**Entschuldigung! Herr Ober!/ Bedienung!**
I didn't order . . .	**Ich habe kein . . . bestellt.**
Another (bottle of/glass of) . . .	**Noch (eine Flasche/ein Glas) . . .**
More (bread/wine/water), please.	**Noch etwas (Brot/Wein/Wasser), bitte.**
The food is (cold/underdone).	**Das Essen ist (kalt/roh).**
Thank you, the food was very nice.	**Danke, das Essen war sehr gut.**

Für wen ist das (Steak/ die Suppe/das Hähnchen)?	Who is the (steak/soup/ chicken) for?
Ist alles in Ordnung?	Is everything OK?
Wie ist (das Fleisch/das Dessert)?	How is the (meat/dessert)?
Darf es noch etwas sein?	Would you like anything else?
Hat es Ihnen geschmeckt?	Did you enjoy it?

Paying

I'd like to pay.	**Ich möchte zahlen.**
The check, please.	**Die Rechnung, bitte.**
Do you take credit cards?	**Nehmen Sie Kreditkarten?**
There is a mistake, I think.	**Ich glaube, da ist ein Fehler.**
We didn't have any (beer/dessert).	**Wir hatten (kein Bier/keinen Nachtisch).**
Keep the change.	**Stimmt so.**

Menu guide

Vorspeise	appetizer
Hauptspeise/Hauptgericht	main dish
Beilage	side dish
Nachspeise/Dessert/Nachtisch	dessert
Tagesgedeck	set menu
Tagesgericht	special
Spezialität des Hauses	specialty of the house
Touristenmenü	tourist menu

Main ways of cooking

gekocht	boiled
gebraten	fried
gegrillt	grilled/broiled
gedämpft	sautéed
gefüllt	filled
gedünstet	steamed
geräuchert	smoked
gewürzt	spicy
hausgemacht	homemade
Jägerart	served in red wine sauce with mushrooms

Sound Check

Eisdiele, Konditorei: the "**ei**" sound sounds like "ai" or "aye" in English

Language works

Ordering a meal

1 Finding a table
- ■ Guten Tag, einen Tisch für drei Personen, bitte.
- □ Einen Moment, bitte. Sie müssen zehn Minuten warten.

How long do you have to wait?

2 Ordering German food
- ■ Die Speisekarte, bitte.
- □ Schön!
  a few minutes later
  Haben Sie schon gewählt?
- ■ Ja, ich möchte bestellen.
- □ Wir haben ein Tagesgericht. Möchten Sie das?
- ■ Können Sie das empfehlen?
- □ Das ist sehr gut. Hähnchen mit Reis.
- ■ Gut, das nehme ich.

What does the waitress recommend? Is today's special pork roast, chicken or beef?

3 Ordering something to drink
- ■ Ich nehme einen Käseteller.
- □ Und was trinken Sie?
- ■ Weißwein, bitte.
- ■ Ein Glas oder eine Flasche?
- ■ Eine Flasche, bitte.

What choice do you have to make?

4 Paying for your meal
- ■ Hat es Ihnen geschmeckt?
- □ Ja, das Essen war sehr gut.
- ■ Darf es noch etwas sein?
- □ Nein, danke. Ich möchte zahlen.

The waitress wants to know if you want to pay: true/false?

At a street stall

5 Trying a German sausage
- ■ Eine Bockwurst, bitte.
- □ Mit Senf oder Ketchup?
- ■ Ohne, bitte. Aber mit Brot.
(**ohne** = without)

What are the options?

6 Getting a slice of pizza
- ■ Ich möchte ein Stück Pizza, bitte.
- □ Das macht vier Mark achtzig. Besteck ist da drüben.

Where do you get the cutlery?

Ordering coffee and cake

7 In the cafeteria
- ■ Entschuldigung, ist hier Selbstbedienung?
- □ Ja, das ist richtig.
- ■ Und wo sind die Tabletts?
- □ Da drüben.

Is it self-service?

Try it out

Matching things

Match the words.
1 red wine
2 a cup of coffee
3 potato salad
4 fish
5 apple cake
6 mixed salad

a **Gemischter Salat**
b **Apfelkuchen**
c **Kartoffelsalat**
d **Rotwein**
e **Fisch**
f **eine Tasse Kaffee**

CÄNSTÄTTER GARTEN
Das Volksfestrestaurant

Wir empfehlen im Bistro:

- Penne Nudeln mit Gemüse-
  bolognese und Parmesan   DM 8,50

- Frische Pizza mit Gemüse-,
  Spinat- oder Champignonfüllung
  und Mozarella überbacken   100 gr. 2,58DM

- Grünkernbratling mit Gewürztofu-
  Champignonfüllung und Mozarella
  überbacken   DM 6,90

- Hirsebratling mit süß-saurem
  Thay-Gemüse und Gouda
  überbacken   DM 5,50

Wordsearch

Can you make ten words from these?

Weiß-	-chen
Rot-	-deln
Schweine-	-eis
Apfel-	-wein
Fla-	-saft
Hähn-	-braten
Nu-	-kartoffeln
Appe-	-kohl
Erdbeer-	-sche
Brat-	-tit

As if you were there

Ordering food
- (Ask for the menu, please)
- □ **Bitte schön.**
- (Say that you would like to order)
- □ **Was bekommen Sie?**
- (Ask if she can recommend anything)
- □ **Ja, der Bratfisch mit Kartoffel-salat ist gut.**
- (You don't like fish, so say thank you and order a pork chop with potatoes and a small salad)

- □ **Hat es Ihnen geschmeckt?**
- (Say that the food was good and that you would like to pay)

Menu reader

Aal eel
Aal in Gelee jellied eel
alkoholfreie Getränke non-alcoholic drinks
alkoholische Getränke alcoholic drinks
Altbier bitter beer
Apfelkuchen apple cake

Apfelkuchen mit Sahne apple cake with whipped cream
Apfelreis apple rice pudding
Apfelsaft apple juice
Apfelschorle apple juice mixed with mineral water
Apfelstrudel apple strudel
Apfelwein apple wine
Auslesewein medium dry wine made with late grapes

Austern oysters
Beefsteak mit Zwiebelringen beefsteak with onions
Beefsteak Tartare raw beef fillet
Beilagen side dishes
Berliner doughnut
Berliner Schloßpunsch punch with rum or brandy
Berliner Weiße light ale with raspberry juice
Berner Platte sauerkraut with various cooked meats
Bienenstich honey and almond cake
Bier beer
Birnen, Bohnen und Speck stew with pears, beans, bacon
Blauer Karpfen blue carp
Blaukraut red cabbage
Blumenkohl cauliflower
Blutwurst type of sausage (similar to blood pudding)
Bockbier strong malt beer
Bockwurst large frankfurter
Bohnen beans
Bouletten hamburgers
Bowle punch
Braten roast meat
Bratfisch mit Kartoffelsalat fried fish with potato salad
Bratkartoffeln fried potatoes
Bratwurst grilled sausage
Bratwurst im Schlafrock sausage roll
Bremer Klaben Bremen sweet

bread
Brotsuppe bread soup
(Franconian style)
Buttermilch buttermilk
Cola cola
Currywurst grilled sausage with
curry and ketchup
Dampfnudeln steamed dumplings
Dillsoße dill sauce
Dorsch cod
Eis ice cream
Eis mit Sahne ice cream with
whipped cream
Eisbein pig's foot
Ente duck
Erbsen peas
Erdbeeren strawberries
Espresso espresso
Fanta lemonade
Fasan mit Weinkraut pheasant
with sauerkraut cooked in wine
Fisch fish
Fischfrikadellen fish cakes
Fleischgerichte meat dishes
Fleischpflanzerl meatballs
Fleischsalat meat salad
Fondue hot melted cheese dip
with bread, or meat cubes fried
in fat
Forelle trout
Frankfurter Kranz Frankfurt
coffee cake
Frikadelle meatball
Frucht nach Jahreszeit seasonal
fruit
Fruchtsaft fruit juice
Gans goose
Geflügel poultry
Geflügelsalat chicken salad
Gefüllte Kalbshaxe stuffed veal
shanks
Gefüllte Tomaten stuffed
tomatoes
Gefüllter Krautkopf stuffed
cabbage
Gemischter Salat mixed salad
Gemüse und Beilagen
vegetables and side dishes
Gemüsesuppe vegetable soup
Geschmorte Rindsleber braised
liver
Getränke drinks

Glühwein mulled wine
Götterspeise jelly
Grieß semolina
Grüne Bohnen green beans
Grüner Salat lettuce/green salad
Gulasch mit Nudeln goulash with
pasta
Gurkensalat cucumber salad
Hackbraten meatloaf
Hackfleisch mince
Hähnchen chicken
Hähnchen mit Reis chicken with
rice
Hamburger Aalsuppe eel soup
from Hamburg
Handkäs country cheese
Hase hare
Haselnußtorte hazelnut cake
Hasenpfeffer hare or rabbit stew
Hauptspeisen main courses
Heilbutt halibut
Heiße Schokolade hot chocolate
Hering herring
Heuriger young wine
Himmel und Erde bacon and
meat casserole with apple sauce
Holländische Soße hollandaise
sauce
Hummer lobster
Kabeljau cod
Kaffee coffee

Kaiserschmarren

Käsespätzle

Kaiserschmarren scrambled
pancakes
Kaiserschnitzel Kaiser cutlet
Kalbfleisch veal
Kalbsbraten mit Champignons
roast veal with mushrooms
Kalbsfrikassee veal stew
Kalbsschnitzel cordon bleu veal
cutlet with ham and cheese
Karotten carrots

Karpfen carp
Kartoffelbrei mashed potatoes
Kartoffeln potatoes
Kartoffelpuffer potato pancake
Kartoffelsalat potato salad
Kartoffelsuppe potato soup
Käsekuchen cheesecake
Käsespätzle cheese noodles
Käseteller cheese platter
Kassler smoked loin of pork
Kirschwasser kirsch
Klöße dumplings
Knoblauch garlic
Knoblauchbrot garlic bread
Knödel dumplings
Koffeinfreier Kaffee
decaffeinated coffee
Kohl cabbage
Kohlrabi kohlrabi
Kohlroulade cabbage stuffed
with minced meat
Kompott stewed fruit
Königsberger Klopse meatballs
in white caper sauce
Kopfsalat lettuce
Korn distilled grain liquor
Kotelett pork chop
Kotelett mit Bratkartoffeln pork

chop with fried potatoes
Krabben prawns
Kraftbrühe clear broth
Kräuterbutter herb butter
Krebs crab
Kuchen cakes
Kümmelstangen caraway
bread sticks
Kürbis pumpkin
Labskaus thick
stew of minced
meat with
mashed
potatoes
Lammfleisch
lamb
Lammkeule leg
of lamb
Lauch leek
Leber liver
Leberkäs meat loaf made
with liver
Leberknödel liver dumplings
Lebkuchen gingerbread
Leipziger Allerlei Leipzig
vegetable platter
Limonade lemonade
Linsensuppe lentil soup
Linzertorte almond
flan with raspberry
topping
Makrele mackerel
Maluns pasta-filled
cabbage
Malzbier dark, sweet
malt beer
Mamorkuchen marble
cake
Mandeltorte almond
cake
Marinierter Hering
pickled herring
Matjeshering salted
herring

Leberkäs

Maultaschen Swabian ravioli
Maultaschen in Zwiebelsuppe
ravioli with onion sauce
Meeresfrüchte
seafood

Meerettichsoße
horseradish
sauce
Mettwurst smoked
sausage spread
Milchkaffee coffee
with cream
Mineralwasser
mineral water
**Mineralwasser mit
Kohlensäure** carbonated
mineral water
Mineralwasser ohne Kohlensäure
noncarbonated mineral water
Mohnkuchen poppy seed cake
Möhren carrots
Mokka strong, black coffee
Mokka-Nußtorte mocha and nut
cake
Nachspeise dessert
Nachtisch dessert
Nieren kidneys

Nachtisch

Sachertorte

Nudeln pasta
Nudelsalat pasta salad
Obsttorte cake with fruit topping
Ochsenmaulsalat tongue salad
Orangensaft orange juice
Petersiliensoße parsley sauce
Pfannkuchen pancake
Pichelsteiner Eintopf Bavarian stew
Pilsner strong, hoppy lager
Pilze mushrooms
Pizokel tiny, pasta-like dumplings
Pökelfleisch marinated meat
Pommes frites french fries
Preiselbeeren cranberries
Pudding white pudding
Pumpernickel heavy black bread
Pute turkey
Quarkspeise cottage cheese with fruit
Rahmschnitzel cutlet with cream sauce
Reibekuchen/ Rösti potato pancakes
Reis rice

Schnitzel

Rheinischer Sauerbraten Rhineland-style sauerbraten
Rinderbraten roast beef
Rinderschmorbraten in Bier rump of beef in beer
Rindersteak mit Pommes frites steak with french fries
Rollmops pickled herring wrapped around slices of onion
Rosenkohl Brussels sprouts
Rote Grütze red jelly pudding
Rotkohl red cabbage
Rotkrautsalat red cabbage salad
Rotwein red wine
Roulade slice of rolled beef in gravy
Rumtopf rum pot
Sachertorte rich chocolate cake
Salate salads
Salatteller salad platter
Sauerbraten marinated, braised beef
Sauerkraut pickled white cabbage
Schaschlick-Spieß German-style kebabs
Schinken in Burgunder ham in burgundy sauce

Schlagsahne whipped cream
Schmalz goose fat
Schnaps schnapps
Schnecken snails
Schnitzel veal or pork cutlet
Schokoladenpudding mit Vanille-soße chocolate pudding with vanilla sauce
Schokoladentorte chocolate cake
Schwarzwälder Kirschtorte Black Forest cake
Schwarzwälder Rehrücken saddle of venison Black Forest style
Schweinebraten roast pork
Schweinebraten mit Kartoffeln oder Klößen roast pork with potatoes or potato dumplings
Seezunge sole
Sekt sparkling wine
Snuten und Poten pickled pork and sauerkraut
Spargel asparagus
Spätzle Swabian pasta
Speckkartoffeln potatoes with bacon
Spezialitäten specialities
Spinat spinach
Stollen cake with almonds, nuts and dried fruit
Strammer Max raw ham and fried eggs served on rye bread
Streuselkuchen crumble cake
Sülze headcheese
Tafelspitz boiled beef
Tee tea
Tee mit Zitrone/Milch tea with lemon/milk
Thunfisch tuna
Tomate tomato
Tomatensalat tomato salad

Torte cake
Traubensaft grape juice
Vanilleeis mit heißen Himbeeren vanilla ice cream with hot raspberries
Vorspeisen appetizers
Wein wine
Weinschorle spritzer
Weißwein white wine
Weißwurst veal sausage
Weizenbier light beer, brewed with wheat
Wurst sausage
Zwiebel onion
Zwiebelkuchen onion tart

Schwarzwälder kirschtorte

Schweinebraten

Entertainment and leisure

Germany is a country of major cultural festivals and sports events of international importance and renown. In cities like Berlin and Munich, festival follows festival, but even the smallest and most insignificant towns have full cultural calendars. Germans take their culture very seriously – almost as seriously as they take their leisure time, which they pack with countless activities. The result is that visitors to Germany are never at a loss for something to do, whatever their taste or wherever in the country they are.

❗ Do you have an entertainment guide?
● **Haben Sie einen Veranstaltungskalender?**

❗ How much is the admission fee?
● **Was kostet der Eintritt?**

Movies

Although Germany has developed film-dubbing to a fine art, all the major cities have theaters where English-language films can be seen in the original. There are three major film festivals: The Berlin Film Festival every February competes with Venice and Cannes, and its Golden Bear awards are coveted by the world's best performers and directors. Munich has a lesser-known summer film festival of great charm and without the Cannes glitz, while Saarbrücken's Max Ophüls film festival is an insider tip for aficionados.

Folk festivals

Every community has at least two annual festivals, and some have several. Carnival – or *Fasching*, as it's known in the South – is celebrated with gusto in the week leading up to Lent, and this is when the locals let their hair down. Summer festivals usually have themes attached to them (the river jousting in Ulm, for instance). Every village boasting a vineyard has an autumn wine festival, while some of the city ones (Stuttgart, for instance) are staggering affairs. Bavaria's summer festivals are usually centered on beer, climaxing with Munich's famous Oktoberfest (which actually begins in September).

Art galleries and museums

It's a poor town indeed that doesn't have its art gallery or local natural history museum. Some of the most unlikely places have some of the most interesting museums – the Herkomer art gallery, for instance, in Landsberg, on the Romantic Route. Cities like Berlin, Cologne, Hamburg and Munich have art galleries that rank among the world's best.

Music and opera

The Richard Wagner opera festival in Bayreuth is world famous, but there are literally hundreds of smaller seasons of concert music, opera and ballet which offer comparable quality and at lower prices. Munich's annual opera festival competes with Bayreuth for sheer star attraction, although castle courtyards throughout the country hold summer opera and music festivals where atmosphere makes up for the lack of crowd-pulling names. Every church with an organ has an annual festival of recitals, most of them in the summer months.

! When does the performance start?
● **Wann fängt die Vorstellung an?**

Sport

Germany is one of the world's leading sporting nations, and every ballgame imaginable – even cricket – is played to international standard. Berlin, Cologne, Dresden, Frankfurt, Hamburg, Munich and Nuremberg all have premier-league soccer clubs playing in splendid grounds, where tickets are readily available for all but the most hotly contested matches, usually local derbies. The star side Bayern Munich plays in Munich's Olympic stadium, so a visit to a match there can be combined with a tour of the futuristic Olympic site. Munich is also the venue of one of the world's leading tennis tournaments, the Grand Slam, but Hamburg and Stuttgart are equally important stops on the international tennis circuit. Public tennis courts are everywhere, and although there is usually no problem booking a court, the fees are relatively high. After a late start, golf is taking an ever-tighter hold of Germany, although there are still very few public courses and visitors usually need to show a foreign club membership and a handicap in order to play. Proof of proficiency is also required by most of the boatyards which rent out dinghies and cabin-cruisers on the coast and on all the inland lakes, and if you want to go horseback riding you'll probably be asked to show your prowess before going out on any of the pretty bridle paths and gallops which crisscross Germany. Anglers must obtain a license (usually from the local tourist board) before casting a line into the country's

well-stocked rivers and lakes, and the penalties for poaching are almost medieval in severity. The uplands and southern Alps, however, are open to everybody, with very few restrictions on hikers and climbers. Climbers, though, should always touch base with local mountaineering clubs (through regional tourist offices) before tackling the higher peaks. Germany's mountain walking is magnificent, the cross-country ski trails are endless and the alpine skiing is as challenging as anywhere in Europe. Cyclists can rent mountain bikes at every Alpine resort, while the German railways, the Deutsche Bahn, rent out bicycles at more than 300 railway stations, at half-price if you travel there by train. Cyclists are privileged road users in most German cities, where cycle paths are constantly being extended. Garmisch-Partenkirchen – site of the 1936 Winter Olympics – is the country's number-one ski center, with year-round skiing on the glacier atop the town's own mountain, the Zugspitze, Germany's highest peak (9,731 ft). But resorts to rival Garmisch-Partenkirchen are to be found all along the mountain ranges which mark Germany's southern border – from the southern slopes of the Black Forest near Switzerland to the alpine peaks which ring Berchtesgaden in the far south-eastern corner of Bavaria. Lower-cost winter vacations can be recommended in the little-known Bavarian Forest, Franconia's Fichtelgebirge, the Vogelsberg and Eifel regions, the Harz and, of course, the Black Forest. They are summertime destinations, too, when the thick fir forests offer shady walking, and the mountain lakes are warm enough to swim in. Every resort has its own open-air swimming pool, and many – such as the Alpamare in Bavaria's Bad Tölz – are of almost Disneyland proportions.

❗ Where can I play tennis?
Wo kann ich Tennis spielen?

And for the children

One of Europe's largest theme parks, the Haßloch Holidaypark, is located on Germany's "Wine Route," between Neustadt and Speyer. The Freizeitpark Tripsdrill, twelve miles south of Heilbronn, Wiesbaden's Taunus Wonderland and the leisure parks at Steinau an der Straße (a "must" destination for families in search of the roots of the Grimm fairy tales) and Ziegenhagen (between Göttingen and Kassel) also attract big crowds.

Phrasemaker

Organizing your entertainment

Do you have (an entertainment guide/a map of the town)?	**Haben Sie (einen Veranstaltungs- kalender/einen Stadtplan)?**
Where is the (museum/gallery/ castle/church/theater/ movie theater/stadium/pool/ sports ground), please?	**Wo ist (das Museum/die Galerie/ das Schloß/die Kirche/ das Theater/das Kino/das Stadion/das Schwimmbad/ die Sportanlage)?**

Getting more information

We'd like to take a trip.	**Wir möchten eine Fahrt machen.**
How much is the entrance fee for (adults/children)?	**Was kostet der Eintritt für (Erwachsene/Kinder)?**
Is there a concession?	**Gibt es Ermäßigung?**
What is there to (do/see) here?	**Was gibt es hier zu (tun/sehen)?**
Is there a (guided tour/ bus tour)?	**Gibt es eine (Führung/Bustour)?**
Are there any (movie theaters/ discos/nightclubs) here?	**Gibt es hier (Kinos/Diskos/ Nachtklubs)?**
Can you recommend a restaurant?	**Können Sie bitte ein Restaurant empfehlen?**
Is there anything for children to do?	**Gibt es hier etwas für Kinder?**

Getting in

When does (it/the performance) start?	**Wann fängt (es/die Vorstellung) an?**
When does it finish?	**Wann ist es zuende?**
How long is the (tour/movie/sightseeing tour/match)?	**Wie lange dauert (die Fahrt/der Film/die Besichtigung/das Spiel)?**
Where do I get the tickets, please?	**Wo bekomme ich die Karten, bitte?**
Do you need tickets?	**Braucht man Eintrittskarten?**
Are there any tickets?	**Gibt es noch Karten?**
Do you have any tickets?	**Haben Sie Karten?**
How much is it?	**Was kostet das?**
Where does the (bus/boat/train) leave from?	**Wo fährt (der Bus/das Boot/der Zug) ab?**
Is it also in English?	**Ist es auch auf Englisch?**
What are the opening hours?	**Wie sind die Öffnungszeiten?**
Das Museum ist (am Marktplatz/im Zentrum/in der Bahnhofsstraße).	The museum is in (the market square/the center/Station Street).
Es gibt zwei (Theater/Kinos).	There are two (theaters/movie theaters).
Wofür interessieren Sie sich?	What are you interested in?
Eine (Karte/Familienkarte) kostet fünfzehn Mark.	A (ticket/family ticket) is 15 marks.
Ja, für (Studenten/Kinder/Rentner).	Yes, for (students/children/seniors).
Die Vorstellung (fängt um sieben Uhr an/geht bis zehn Uhr/dauert zwei Stunden).	The performance (starts at 7 pm/finishes at 10 pm/lasts two hours).
Sie können die Karten (hier/im Museum/am Schalter) kaufen.	You can buy the tickets (here/at the museum/at the counter)
Es gibt eine Führung.	There's a guided tour.
Der Bus fährt vom (Hauptbahnhof/Rathausplatz) ab.	The bus leaves from the (main station/town hall square).
Er ist (frei/besetzt).	It is (free/taken).
Veranstaltungskalender	entertainment guide

At the museum

(One/two) tickets, please.	**(Eine/zwei) Eintrittskarten, bitte.**
For (Saturday/tomorrow).	**Für (Samstag/morgen).**
Have you got any catalogs?	**Haben Sie Kataloge?**
Do you have this in English?	**Haben Sie das auf Englisch?**

At the theater and the movies

When does the performance start?	**Wann beginnt die Vorstellung?**
What seats do you have left?	**Was für Plätze haben Sie noch?**
Are the seats numbered?	**Sind die Plätze numeriert?**
Is this place taken?	**Ist dieser Platz besetzt?**
Will there be a break?	**Gibt es eine Pause?**
Where can I buy a program?	**Wo kann ich ein Programm kaufen?**
Does the film have subtitles?	**Hat der Film Untertitel?**

Um acht Uhr.	At eight o'clock.
Wir haben noch Plätze (im Parkett/auf dem Balkon).	We have seats (in the orchestra/in the balcony).
Sie können sitzen, wo Sie möchten.	You can sit where you like.
Die Pause ist zwanzig Minuten.	The break will be 20 minutes.
Hier/dort drüben.	Here/over there.

At the swimming pool and on the beach

Can I use the hotel pool?	**Kann ich das Hotelschwimmbad benutzen?**
Do I need (change/a bathing cap)?	**Brauche ich (Wechselgeld/eine Badekappe)?**
I'd like to rent a/an (umbrella/deck chair/beach chair).	**Ich möchte einen (Sonnenschirm/Liegestuhl/Strandkorb) mieten.**
How long can I stay?	**Wie lange kann ich im Bad bleiben?**
Where are the (locker rooms/hair dryers/showers/lockers/restrooms), please?	**Wo sind die (Umkleidekabinen/Haartrockener/Duschen/Schließfächer/Toiletten)?**
ladies/gentlemen	**Damen/Herren**

Sports

Where can I (go swimming/ play tennis)?	**Wo kann ich (schwimmen gehen/ Tennis spielen)?**
I'd like to rent (a racket/ water skis).	**Ich möchte (einen Schläger/ Wasserskier) leihen.**
I'd like to take (skiing/sailing/ horseback riding) lessons.	**Ich möchte (Skiunterricht/ Segelunterricht/Reitunterricht) nehmen.**

Ja, das bekommen Sie hier.	Yes, you get it here.
(Eine/zwei) Stunde(n).	(One/two) hours.
Die sind (hier/unten/oben/ rechts/links).	They are (here/downstairs/ upstairs/on the right/on the left).

Things to do or see

Ausstellung	exhibition
Disko	disco
Feuerwerk	fireworks
Fußballspiel	soccer match
Galerie	gallery
Golfplatz	golf course
Kino	movies
Konzert	concert
Museum	museum
Nachtclub	nightclub
Theater	theater
Stadion	stadium
Schwimmbad	swimming pool
Show	show
Sporthalle	sports hall
Tennisspiel	tennis match

Signs

Ausgang	exit		**Herren**	Gentlemen
Balkon	balcony		**Parkett**	orchestra
Bar	bar		**Rang**	circle
Damen	Ladies		**Toiletten**	restrooms
Garderobe	cloakroom		**Treppe**	stairs

On a trip

Excuse me, is this seat free?	**Entschuldigung, ist hier noch frei?**
May I smoke here?	**Darf ich hier rauchen?**
Is this waiter service?	**Ist hier Bedienung?**
When do we continue?	**Wann geht es weiter?**
Where do I pay?	**Wo muß ich bezahlen?**

Dieser Platz ist (frei/besetzt).	This seat is (free/taken).
Hier dürfen Sie nicht rauchen.	You mustn't smoke here.
Hier dürfen sie rauchen.	You can smoke here.
Sie können hier aussteigen.	You can get off here.
Fahrkarten, bitte.	Tickets, please.
(Beim Fahrer/Am Schalter) zahlen.	Pay (the driver/at the counter).

Sunbathing

Badetuch	beach towel	**Sonnencreme**	suntan lotion
Handtuch	hand towel	**Sonnenschirm**	umbrella
Liegestuhl	deck chair	**Strandkorb**	beach chair
Sonnenbrille	sunglasses		

Sports

Abfahrtslauf	downhill skiing	**Surfen**	surfing
Bergsteigen	climbing	**Tennis**	tennis
Geländelauf	cross-country	**Volleyball**	volleyball
Golf	golf	**Wandern**	walking
Reiten	horseback riding	**Wasserski**	waterskiing
Segeln	sailing	**Windsurfen**	windsurfing

Sports equipment

Bälle	balls	**Stiefel**	boots
Golfschläger	golf clubs	**Surfbrett**	surfboard
Segelboot	sailboat	**Tennisschläger**	tennis racket
Skier	skis	**Wasserskier**	waterskis

Sound Check

Student: "**st**" at the beginning of a word sounds "sht"
Restaurant: "**st**" in the middle of the word is "st"

Language works

Getting information

1 At the tourist office
- **Entschuldigung, wo ist die Nationalgalerie?**
- ☐ **Sie ist am Bahnhof, in der Ottostraße.**
- **Wie sind die Öffnungszeiten, bitte?**
- ☐ **Von neun bis sechzehn Uhr.**
- **Danke schön.**

How many hours is the gallery open for?

2 A guided tour
- **Wir möchten eine Stadtrundfahrt machen. Wie lange dauert die, bitte?**
- ☐ **Zwei Stunden. Sie kostet vierzig Mark.**
- **Gut. Wo bekomme ich die Karten?**
- ☐ **Sie können die Karten hier kaufen.**

The trip takes: one/two/three hours.

3 Catching the bus
- **Wo fährt der Bus ab?**
- ☐ **Vom Rathausmarkt.**
- **Wann, bitte?**
- ☐ **Jede volle Stunde.**

The bus leaves every other hour: true/false?

4 An evening out
- **Was kosten die Karten für Aida?**
- ☐ **Achtzig Mark.**
- **Wie lange dauert die Vorstellung?**
- ☐ **Vier Stunden. Sie fängt um sechs Uhr an und geht bis zehn Uhr.**

It's a long opera. When does it start and finish?

5 At the museum
- **Eine Eintrittskarte, bitte. Gibt es Ermäßigung für Studenten?**
- ☐ **Leider nicht. Acht Mark, bitte.**
- **Bitte schön. Haben sie Kataloge auf Englisch?**
- ☐ **Selbstverständlich.**

Is eight marks the full fee or do you get a discount?

6 Buying tickets for a show
- **Guten Abend! Wann beginnt die nächste Vorstellung, bitte?**
- ☐ **Um acht Uhr.**
- **Was für Plätze haben Sie noch?**
- ☐ **Wir haben noch Plätze im Parkett.**

(**nächste** = next)

Is the next performance in the afternoon or the evening?

Playing sports

7 At the swimming pool
- **Guten Tag. Zwei Erwachsene, bitte.**
- ☐ **Zehn Mark vierzig, bitte.**
- **Wie lange kann ich im Bad bleiben?**

□ **Zwei Stunden.**
■ **Und wo sind die Umkleide-kabinen?**
□ **Die sind unten.**

How much is a ticket?
The locker rooms are on the left:
true/false?

On a trip

8 Where to pay
■ **Wo muß ich bezahlen?**
□ **Beim Fahrer.**

Do you buy the ticket at a counter?

9 Asking for a seat
■ **Entschuldigung, ist hier noch frei?**
□ **Tut mir leid, der Platz ist besetzt.**

Are you lucky or is the seat taken?

10 Having a break on a bus tour
■ **Sie können hier aussteigen. Wir machen dreißig Minuten Pause.**
□ **Wann geht es weiter?**
■ **Um vier Uhr.**

Are you allowed to leave the bus?

Try it out

As if you were there

Getting some information from the tourist office
■ (Ask where the "Kölner Dom" is)
□ **Der ist im Zentrum.**
■ (Inquire about the opening hours)
□ **Von zehn bis siebzehn Uhr.**
■ (You would like to take a tour of the city. Ask where the bus leaves from)
□ **Um elf Uhr, vom Hauptbahnhof.**
■ (Ask how long the tour takes)
□ **Drei Stunden mit Pause.**

■ (Ask where you can buy the tickets)
□ **Sie können die Karten hier kaufen.**

Jumbled dialogue

Can you put the sentences in order?
□ **Der Bus fährt vom Rathausmarkt ab.**
■ **Wie lange dauert die Fahrt?**
■ **Wo kann ich die Karten kaufen?**
□ **Ja, dreißig Minuten.**
■ **Wo fährt der Bus ab?**
□ **Beim Fahrer.**
□ **Drei Stunden.**
■ **Gibt es eine Pause?**

Puzzle

Find ten words related to tourist information. Two examples are given already. How about the other eight?

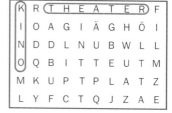

Emergencies

English has always been the primary foreign language taught in virtually all west-German secondary schools and rapidly took over from Russian in the east after the *Wende* in 1989. Consequently, most younger Germans can speak and understand at least some English and a surprisingly large number of older citizens, particularly in urban areas, also cope well with the language. Telephone operators are encouraged to become proficient in English, and for those handling calls abroad it's a prerequisite.

Many local radio stations carry news in English, and a fortnightly English-language news magazine, produced by Bavarian TV, is networked to most of the country. Berlin, Hamburg and Munich have English-language newspapers and magazines carrying information for visitors. All tourist offices carry information brochures in English. Popular German newspapers and magazines (such as *Bild* and *Bunte*) are easy to read for anyone with basic German.

All the major cities and many towns have pharmacies where well-known brands of foreign pharmaceuticals are stocked and where the staff speak English. Consult telephone books or the yellow pages under *Internationale Apotheken* (international pharmacies). Pharmacies are easily identified by a large red sign reading Apotheke or simply A. They are not to be confused with *Drogerien*, which will sell a wide range of toiletries and other related products, but are not allowed to dispense medicine.

In general, postage stamps can only be obtained at post offices (open normal shop hours, but with a lunch-time break of an hour or so), but some stationers sell them. Long-distance telephone calls booked at a post office counter are charged an additional fee. The easiest and cheapest way to phone is by using a telephone card, obtainable at all post offices and at some newspaper stands. Coin-operated telephones are becoming a rarity, so it's advisable to carry a telephone card.

Emergency medical aid can be obtained by dialing 112, anywhere in the country. The police emergency number is 110.

❗ Where is the nearest pharmacy, please?
● Wo ist die nächste Apotheke, bitte?

Phrasemaker

General phrases

Can you help me?	**Können Sie mir helfen?**
Excuse me!	**Entschuldigung!**
Hello there!	**Hallo!**
Help!	**Hilfe!**
I'll call the police!	**Ich rufe die Polizei!**
It's urgent!	**Es ist dringend!**
Leave me alone!	**Laß mich in Ruhe!**
Is there someone here who speaks English?	**Spricht hier jemand Englisch?**
Thank you!	**Danke schön!**

Finding places in case of an emergency

Where is the nearest . . . ?	**Wo ist . . . ?**
pharmacy	**die nächste Apotheke**
doctor	**der nächste Arzt**
hospital	**das nächste Krankenhaus**
emergency room	**die nächste Unfallstation**
lost and found	**das nächste Fundbüro**
garage	**die nächste Autowerkstatt**
gas station	**die nächste Tankstelle**
telephone	**das nächste Telefon**
police station	**die nächste Polizeiwache**

Getting help   St. Marienhospital

I need . . .	**Ich brauche . . .**
a doctor	**einen Arzt**
medicine	**Medizin**
an ambulance	**einen Krankenwagen**
first-aid kit	**einen Verbandskasten**
adhesive bandage	**ein Pflaster**
headache tablets	**Kopfschmerztabletten**
painkillers	**Schmerztabletten**
cough medicine	**Hustensaft**

Have you got anything for . . .	**Haben Sie etwas gegen . . .**
a headache	**Kopfschmerzen**
fever	**Fieber**
hay fever	**Heuschnupfen**
allergies	**Allergien**
burns	**Verbrennungen**
stomachaches	**Magenschmerzen**
indigestion	**Verdauungsbeschwerden**
cold	**Erkältung**
sickness and nausea	**Übelkeit**
back pain	**Rückenschmerzen**

insomnia	**Schlaflosigkeit**
cough	**Husten**
toothache	**Zahnschmerzen**
pain	**Schmerzen**

At the pharmacy

Excuse me, I need . . .	**Entschuldigung, ich brauche . . .**
Have you got something for . . . a headache/a cough/an infection?	**Haben Sie etwas gegen . . . Kopfschmerzen/Husten/ Infektion?**
Can you recommend anything?	**Können Sie etwas empfehlen?**
Have you got anything (cheaper/ stronger)?	**Haben Sie etwas (Billigeres/ Stärkeres)?**
Is it a strong medicine?	**Ist das Medikament stark?**
Does it contain . . . penicillin?	**Enthält es . . . Penizillin?**
How often do I have to take it?	**Wie oft muß ich das nehmen?**
Does it have side effects?	**Hat es Nebenwirkungen?**
	Brauche ich ein Rezept?

Möchten Sie (Tabletten/Creme/ Saft/Tropfen) eine (große/ kleine) (Packung/Flasche)?	Would you like (tablets/cream/ liquid/drops) a (small/big) (packet/bottle)?
Nehmen Sie das (einmal/ zweimal/dreimal) täglich morgens/mittags/abends	Take this (once/twice/three) times a day in the morning/at lunchtime/ in the evening
mit Wasser (vor/nach) dem Essen	with water (before/after) the meal
Das ist rezeptpflichtig.	You need a prescription for that.

Parts of the body

ankle	**der Fußknöchel**	knee	**das Knie**
arm	**der Arm**	leg	**das Bein**
back	**der Rücken**	liver	**die Leber**
chest	**die Brust**	mouth	**der Mund**
chin	**das Kinn**	nails	**die Nägel**
ear	**das Ohr**	neck	**das Genick**
elbow	**der Ellbogen**	nose	**die Nase**
eyes	**die Augen**	shoulder	**die Schulter**
fingers	**die Finger**	stomach	**der Magen**
foot	**der Fuß**	teeth	**die Zähne**
hair	**das Haar**	thigh	**der Ober- schenkel**
hand	**die Hand**		
head	**der Kopf**	throat	**der Hals**
hip	**die Hüfte**	toes	**die Zehen**
kidneys	**die Nieren**	tooth	**der Zahn**

At the doctor/dentist

My head . . . hurts.	**Mein Kopf . . . tut weh.**
I'm in a lot of pain.	**Ich habe starke Schmerzen.**
Could you give me a prescription?	**Können Sie mir ein Rezept geben?**
Could you transfer me to a specialist?	**Können Sie mich an einen Spezialisten überweisen?**
I can't move/feel my . . .	**Ich kann mein . . . nicht bewegen/fühlen**
my neck/finger/leg	**mein Genick/meinen Finger/ mein Bein**
I've (cut/burnt) myself.	**Ich habe mich (geschnitten/ verbrannt).**
I've been bitten by a dog.	**Ein Hund hat mich gebissen.**
I've been bitten by an insect.	**Ein Insekt hat mich gestochen.**
It hurts here.	**Es tut hier weh.**
I'm allergic to (antibiotics/ animals).	**Ich bin gegen (Antibiotika/Tiere) allergisch.**
I'm (diabetic/pregnant).	**Ich bin (Diabetiker/schwanger).**
I've lost a filling.	**Ich habe eine Plombe verloren.**

Wie geht es Ihnen?	How are you?
Wo tut es weh?	Where does it hurt?
Machen Sie sich bitte frei.	Please undress.

Ich muß Sie untersuchen.	I have to examine you.
Haben Sie einen internationalen Krankenschein?	Do you have an international health insurance certificate?
Es ist nicht schlimm.	It is not serious.
Der Knochen ist gebrochen.	The bone is broken.
Sie müssen operiert werden.	You need an operation.
Ich mache Ihnen eine Plombe.	I'll put in a filling.
Ich muß den Zahn ziehen.	I'll have to take this tooth out.
Sie müssen (Medizin nehmen/ sich hinlegen).	You have to (take medicine/ lie down).
Sie dürfen nicht (schwimmen/ rauchen/essen/aufstehen).	You mustn't (swim/smoke/ eat/get up).

At the police station

I've lost my (passport/luggage/ bag).
My (ticket/jewelry/suitcase/ car/money) was stolen.
I was mugged.
I had an accident.

Ich habe (meinen Paß/mein Gepäck/meine Tasche) verloren.
Mein (Ticket/Schmuck/Koffer/ Auto/Geld) wurde gestohlen.
Ich bin überfallen worden.
Ich hatte einen Unfall.

Wie ist (Ihr Name/Ihre Adresse)?
Wie heißt Ihr Hotel?
(Wann/Wo) ist das passiert?
Bitte füllen Sie das Formular aus!

What's your (name/address)?
What's the name of your hotel?
(When/Where) did that happen?
Please fill out this form!

At the lost and found

I've lost my (briefcase/wallet/ jacket/shopping bag).

Ich habe (meinen Aktenkoffer/ meine Brieftasche/meine Jacke/ meine Einkaufstasche) verloren.

Was . . . handed in?
It's (big/small/red/blue/ black/white/brown/ expensive/made of leather/ wool/cotton).

Ist . . . abgegeben worden?
Es ist (groß/klein/rot/blau/ schwarz/weiß/braun/ teuer/aus Leder/ Wolle/Baumwolle).

Sammlungswesen		
Ordnungswidrigkeiten (Bußgeldstelle) Verwarnungsstelle	Aufzugsgruppe 1	Etage 4
Anwohnerparkausweise Taxen, Mietwagen, Güterkraft- verkehr, Verkehrslenkung Marktwesen	Aufzugsgruppe 1	Etage 4
Fundbüro	Aufzugsgruppe 2	Etage P 1

yesterday
(morning
evening
afternoon)
last night/
this morning
in the street/
in the store

gestern
(morgen/ abend/ nachmittag)
gestern abend/ heute morgen
auf der Straße/ im Geschäft

Wann haben Sie . . . verloren?
Wie sieht . . . aus?
Haben Sie einen Ausweis dabei?
Ja, Sie haben Glück.
Nein, tut mir leid. Hier ist nichts abgegeben worden.

When did you lose . . . ?
What does . . . look like?
Have you got an ID on you?
Yes, you are lucky.
No, sorry. Nothing has been handed in.

Valuables

money	**das Geld**		jewelry	**der Schmuck**
wallet	**die Brieftasche**		necklace	**die Kette**
purse	**das Porte- monnaie**		car	**das Auto**
			passport	**der Reisepaß**
handbag	**die Handtasche**		driver's	**der Führer-**
briefcase	**der Aktenkoffer**		license	**schein**
suitcase	**der Koffer**		tickets	**die Karten**

A car breakdown

Could you please help me?	**Könnten Sie mir bitte helfen?**
My car broke down.	**Ich habe eine Panne.**
on the highway A 28	**auf der Autobahn A 28**
. . . kilometers from . . .	**. . . Kilometer von . . .**
I need tools.	**Ich brauche Werkzeug.**
How far is the next . . .	**Wie weit ist die/der/das nächste . . .**
(The engine/steering) isn't working.	**(Der Motor/die Lenkung) funktioniert nicht.**
The brakes aren't working.	**Die Bremsen funktionieren nicht.**
I've run out of gas.	**Ich habe kein Benzin mehr.**
When will it be ready?	**Wann ist es fertig?**

Was ist passiert?	What happened?
Wann . . .?	When . . .?
Wo . . .?	Where . . .?
Sind Sie verletzt?	Are you hurt?

Wie ist (Ihr Name/Ihre Adresse/ Autonummer/Ausweis- nummer)?	What is your (name/address/ license plate number/ passport number)?
Wie ist Ihre Versicherungs- nummer?	What's your insurance number?
Ihre Papiere, bitte.	Show me your papers, please.
Kommen Sie später wieder.	Come back later.

Main car parts

steering wheel	**das Steuerrad**	accelerator	**das Gaspedal**
clutch	**die Kupplung**	radiator	**der Kühler**
windshield	**die Windschutz- scheibe**	windows	**die Scheiben**
		wheels	**die Räder**
wiper	**der Scheiben- wischer**	tires	**die Reifen**
		tools	**das Werkzeug**
brakes	**die Bremsen**		

Sound Check

Krankenhaus: the "**au**" is like the sound in "now"
Verbrennungen: the "**v**" sounds like "f" in English

Language works

At the police station

1 My money was stolen
- **Guten Tag, mein Geld wurde gestohlen.**
- □ **Wo ist das passiert?**
- **Im Hotel.**
- □ **Wie heißt Ihr Hotel?**
- **Hotel zur Post.**

What information do the police ask for?

2 Last night
- **Ich bin überfallen worden.**
- □ **Wann ist das passiert?**
- **Gestern abend.**
- □ **Bitte füllen Sie das Formular aus.**
(**gestern abend** = last night)

What are you asked to do?

Losing things

3 At the lost and found
- **Ich habe meinen Aktenkoffer verloren. Haben Sie ihn gefunden?**
- □ **Wie sieht der Koffer aus?**
- **Er ist klein, braun und aus Leder. Ist er abgegeben worden?**
- □ **Wie ist ihr Name?**
- **Gary Atkinson.**
- □ **Ja, Sie haben Glück.**

The briefcase is black, rather big, made of leather: true/false?

Feeling sick

4 Getting some headache tablets
- **Entschuldigung, ich brauche Kopfschmerztabletten. Können Sie etwas empfehlen?**
- □ **Diese Tabletten sind gut. Möchten Sie eine große oder eine kleine Packung?**
- **Eine große, bitte.**
(**gut** = good)

What can you choose from?

5 Feeling nauseous
- **Haben Sie etwas gegen Übelkeit?**
- □ **Ja hier, bitte. Nehmen Sie das dreimal täglich vor dem Essen.**
- **Danke schön.**

What is the procedure?

6 At the doctor's office
- **Guten Tag, Herr Doktor.**
- □ **Wie geht es Ihnen? Wo tut es weh?**
- **Mein Rücken tut weh.**
- □ **Machen Sie sich bitte frei. Sie müssen sich hinlegen.**

Does the doctor have to examine you? After the examination you should lie down/go swimming.

7 Dealing with the papers
- **Haben Sie einen internationalen Krankenschein?**
- □ **Ja, hier, bitte.**
- **Gut, wo tut es weh?**
- □ **Ich habe Magenschmerzen. Können Sie mir ein Rezept geben?**
- **Natürlich.**

What paper do you have to produce? Will the doctor give you a prescription?

Solving problems

8 A car breakdown
- **Könnten Sie mir bitte helfen?**
- □ **Sind Sie verletzt?**
- **Nein. Ich habe eine Panne. Ich brauche Hilfe.**
- □ **Die nächste Tankstelle ist fünfhundert Meter.**
(**fünfhundert Meter** = 500 meters)

What help will you find 500 meters ahead?

9 Asking for gas
- **Brauchen Sie Benzin?**
- □ **Ja, bitte. Zwanzig Liter.**
(**Liter** = liters)

How much gas do you ask for?
10/ 20/30 liters?

10 An accident
- **Ich hatte einen Unfall. Ich brauche einen Krankenwagen.**
- □ **Sofort. Dort ist ein Telefon.**
(**sofort** = at once, **dort** = there)

The ambulance is on its way/
The other driver is going to call an ambulance.

Try it out

As if you were there

At the pharmacy
- (You have hay fever. Ask if the pharmacist can recommend anything.)
- □ **Ja hier. Möchten Sie Tropfen oder Tabletten?**
- (Say you would like a big packet of tablets.)

At the lost and found
- (Say that you lost your coat and ask if it was handed in.)
- □ **Wie sieht Ihr Mantel aus?**

- (Describe your coat: It is black and made from cotton.)
- □ **Tut mir leid. Hier ist nichts abgegeben worden.**

A car breakdown
- (Ask if the other driver can help you.)
- □ **Natürlich. Sind Sie verletzt?**
- (Say no, but you need tools.)

At the police station
- **Ihr Name, bitte?**
- □ (Say your name.)
- **Ihre Adresse, bitte.**
- □ (Give your address.)
- **Was ist passiert?**
- □ (Say that your car was stolen.)

Do you know the words?

You left your suitcase on the train. Where do you go to get it back?
F _ _ _ _ _ _ _

You need gas. What do you have to look out for?
T _ _ _ _ _ _ _ _ V

You go to the doctor in Germany. What paper do you need?
I _ _ _ _ _ _ _ _ _ _ _ _ V
K _ _ _ _ _ _ _ _ _ _ _

For medicine you don't get over the counter, you need a . . .
R _ _ _ _ _

You can buy medicine in different containers. In a . . . or a . . .
F _ _ _ _ _ _
P _ _ _ _ _ _

Venusberg → | Uni-Kliniken → | ↑ St. Marien-Hospital Kinderkrankenhaus

Language builder

Markt

Actually German is not as complicated as you might think, as you can "get by" with a few basic ideas. Germans are grateful if you make any attempt to learn the language. But if you get really stuck . . . don't worry, as most Germans will love to try out their English on you.

And here is a short introduction to the ways the German language works:

du/Sie

As in many other European languages, there is a polite form "**Sie**" and an informal way "**du**" of addressing people. The "**du**" is used among friends, family and young people. The "**Sie**" is used in formal situations and when you don't know people. So if you address anybody in a public place, use this form. This is a way of showing respect. If in doubt, say "**Sie**."

Verbs and pronouns

to buy/I buy
Again as in many other languages, the verbs are conjugated. That means changing the endings according to the person it refers to.
Here is an example:
Ich kaufe die CD. I buy the CD.
Du kaufst die CD. You buy the CD.

Don't worry if you get the endings wrong. People will still understand you. Here is a table of how the regular verbs work, but then there are quite a few irregular ones. In this book you will find the verbs in the form you are most likely to need them. When you look up a word in the dictionary, you will find it in its basic form, "the infinitive." Almost all German infinitives end in "**-en.**" Then you only have to add the ending as shown here, as long as the verb is regular:
kaufen – to buy

Singular:
ich kaufe   I buy
du kaufst   you buy
er/sie/es kauft   he/she/it buys

Plural:
wir kaufen   we buy
ihr kauft   you buy
sie kaufen   they buy

Articles (the/a)

In German there are three of them:

<u>the</u>
masculine: **der**
feminine: **die**
neuter: **das**

<u>a</u>
masculine: **ein**
feminine: **eine**
neuter: **ein**

examples:
der Bus	the bus
die Straße	the street
das Auto	the car
ein Bus	a bus
eine Straße	a street
ein Auto	a car

The plural form is always "**die**."

examples:
die Männer	the men
die Frauen	the women
die Hotels	the hotels
die Karten	the tickets

Unfortunately these articles are often not very logical, but if you don't get them right, people will still understand you.
When it comes to professions, you will also find that there are masculine and feminine forms of job titles. But they are very easy to understand. The feminine form mostly ends in "**-in**." For example:
der Manager/die Managerin,
der Student/die Studentin,
and for dentists **der Zahnarzt/ die Zahnärztin**.

Possessives (my/your)

In order to identify "whose" something is, you might need:

Mein Name . . . ist Clarke
  My name . . . is Clarke
Wie ist dein/Ihr Name?
  What's your name?
  (informal/formal)
Unser Hotel ist gut.
  Our hotel is good

der Dom, Munich

↑ **Hauptbahnhof**

← 🛣

← **Zentrum**

Question words

It is always very helpful to know how to ask for things. As in English, put the question word mostly at the beginning of a sentence:

Was ist das ?
   What is this?
Wie viele sind da ?
   How many are there?
Wieviel kostet das?
   How much is that?
Wo ist das?
   Where is that?
Wie komme ich zum Bahnhof?
   How do I get to the station?
Wann fährt der Bus?
   When does the bus leave?
Wohin fährt er?
   Where does it go?
Woher kommen Sie?
   Where do you come from?
Wer ist das?
   Who is that?

Sentence structure

If you stick to short sentences, the principle is fairly easy. The structure of a simple sentence is as in English:

subject	verb	object
Ich	**kaufe**	**eine CD.**
I	buy	a CD.
Er	**trinkt**	**ein Bier.**
He	drinks	a beer.

You can build more and more sentences like this. Easy, isn't it?

When you ask for things, the sentence becomes longer, as you have two verbs:

subject	verb 1	object	verb 2
Ich	**möchte**	**eine CD**	**kaufen.**
I	want	a CD	to buy.

If you do have two verbs, you put the main one, which is the one with the meaning, at the end. This verb stays in the infinitive "**-en**" form. The "helping" verb goes to the second position. This one has the ending according to the person.

Plurals

In German there are different ways of forming plurals, so it is best to learn the plural form right away when you learn a new word. The easy thing is, that the plural article is always: "**die.**"

Here are a few examples:

singular	plural
das Foto	**die Foto*s***
die Woche	**die Woch*en***
der Tag	**die Tag*e***
das Kind	**die Kind*er***
das Land	**die Länd*er***
das Zimmer	**die Zimmer**
das Museum	**die Muse*en***

Prepositions

German prepositions are not difficult to learn, . . . as long as you don't use them in a sentence! Depending on the sentence, the articles after a preposition change. But you don't need to worry about that, if you use them on their own and use gestures. Anybody will understand, if you ask: "**rechts oder links,**" right or left, "**vor oder hinter,**" in front of or behind, waving your arms in the respective direction.

So here are a few words to help you along:

vor	in front of
hinter	behind
auf	on
unter	under
von	from
nach	to
neben	next to
zwischen	between
um	around
über	above
in	in
durch	through

Adjectives

As long as you put the adjective, the describing word, at the end of the sentence, this is no problem at all.

Examples:
Die CD ist teuer.
 The CD is expensive.
Das Hotel ist gut.
 The hotel is good.
Das Essen schmeckt fantastisch.
 The food tastes fantastic.

Comparatives

To use comparatives, it is mostly safe just to add "**er**" to the adjective:
Mein Zimmer ist schön.
 My room is nice.
Dein Zimmer ist schöner.
 Your room is nicer.

Berlin ist weit.
 Berlin is far.
Dresden ist weiter.
 Dresden is further.

In order to say that something is too small, or too expensive, all you have to do is to put "**zu**" in front of the adjective:

Das Auto ist zu klein.
 The car is too small.
Das Zimmer ist zu teuer.
 The room is too expensive.

As always, there are a few exceptions to the rules of comparatives. Here are the most common and useful ones:

gut	**besser**
good	better
viel	**mehr**
a lot	more
teuer	**teurer**
expensive	more expensive
hoch	**höher**
high	higher
lang	**länger**
long	longer
kurz	**kürzer**
short	shorter

Answers

Bare necessities

1 For two weeks. Yes
2 Your wife. True.
3 Straight ahead.
4 You ask whether he speaks
English.

As if you were there
- Hallo, wie geht's?
- Wie heißt du?
- Ich heiße . . . Woher kommst du?
- Ich komme aus . . .

Numbers
a Ruth Städing
b Peter Wiese
c Claudia Hauswirt

Getting around

1 On the left. 2 The bus stop is
around the corner. Number nine.
3 A VW Golf. One week. 4 24 marks.
5 You have to fill up yourself. 6 Super.
Super or unleaded. 7 Take the first
street on the right. Hannover is about
100 kilometers away. 8 No, you
have to get the U 1. 9 A round-trip
ticket. It costs 87 marks including
reservation of a seat.
10 The train leaves at 8:17 from platform 14 and arrives at 10:03 in
Munich.

Puzzle
A zurück; Platz; Gleis.
B Wo; geradeaus.

As if you were there
- Wo ist die Touristeninformation,
  bitte?
- Ist das weit?
- Und gibt es hier in der Nähe eine
  Bank?

Somewhere to stay

1 Your name. 620 marks for one
week. 2 You have to sign it. 3 10:00;
9:00. No, they are full. 4 On the first
floor. It does not have a TV. No
because all spaces are full. A wake-up
call. With credit cards but not with
checks. 5 Camper. Four people.
Showers and toilets. On the left.
6 Your membership card for youth
hostels. On the third floor, room 301.

Puzzle
1 Wohnwagen, 2 Speisesaal,
3 Parkplatz, 4 Pension,
5 Zimmerschlüssel, 6 besetzt,
7 Frühstück, 8 Fernseher

Matching sentences
- Für wie viele Nächte?
- □ Eine Woche, bitte.
- Hat das Zimmer Telefon?
- □ Nein, aber einen Fernseher
- Wo gibt es Frühstück?
- □ Im Speisesaal.
- Wie viele Personen sind Sie?
- □ Zwei Erwachsene.
- Haben Sie Zimmer frei?
- □ Alle Zimmer sind belegt.

As if you were there
- □ Ich möchte ein Doppelzimmer und
  ein Einzelzimmer.
- □ Für vier Nächte, bitte.Hat das
  Doppelzimmer ein Telefon?
- □ Mit Dusche, bitte.

Buying things

1 13.80 marks. 2 Wheat bread. 3 In
a jar. 4 To the right. 5 The pants are
the most expensive item and the shirt
is the cheapest. 6 80 pfennigs. The
total is 22.40 marks.
7 One hour. No.

As if you were there
At the newsstand
- Wie viel kostet der
  Kugelschreiber?

- Haben Sie englische Zeitschriften?
- Ich möchte zwei Postkarten.
- Danke. Auf Wiedersehen.

Sending some cards home
- Entschuldigung, wo muss ich mich anstellen?
- Wieviel kostet ein Brief nach Australien?

Adding up
6,35 DM

Word game
zehn, Entschuldigung, ich, Traube, und, nehmen, Größe; new word: Zeitung

Café life

1 Apple cake. 2 A pot or a cup.
3 Chocolate cake.

Dialogue
□ Guten Tag, was bekommen Sie?
■ Ein Stück Apfelkuchen, bitte.
□ Selbstverständlich. Und was trinken Sie?
■ Kaffee, bitte.
□ Kännchen oder Tasse?
■ Eine Tasse, bitte.
□ Kommt sofort.

Missing words
Sie; leid; Tasse; Kännchen; Mineralwasser; sofort.

Which answer matches?
□ Mit Kohlensäure?
□ Ja, Apfelkuchen.
□ Das macht 3,50 DM, bitte.
□ Mineralwasser, Limonade, Cola, . . .

Which one is it?
A Schokolade. B Kirscheis.
C Sahne. D Tut mir leid.
E ein Stück.

Eating out

1 Ten minutes. 2 The day's special. It is chicken. 3 You have to choose between a glass or a bottle of wine.
4 False: The waitress asks whether you liked the food and whether you'd like anything else. 5 You can get the sausage with mustard or ketchup.
6 From over there. 7 Yes.

Matching things
1d; 2f; 3c; 4e; 5b; 6a

Wordsearch

Erdbeereis	Weißwein
Rotkohl	Bratkartoffeln
Flasche	Hähnchen
Appetit	Apfelsaft
Nudeln	Schweinebraten

As if you were there
- Die Speisekarte, bitte.
- Ich möchte bestellen.
- Können Sie etwas empfehlen?
- Danke. Ich möchte ein Kotelett mit Kartoffeln und einen kleinen Salat.
- Ja, das Essen war gut. Ich möchte bitte zahlen.

Entertainment and leisure

1 Seven hours, from nine to four.
2 Two hours. 3 False. 4 It starts at six and finishes at ten. 5 Eight marks is the full fee. 6 In the evening. 7 5,20 marks. False. 8 No, you buy the ticket from the driver. 9 No, the seat is taken. 10 Yes.

As if you were there
- Wo ist der Kölner Dom, bitte?
- Wie sind die Öffnungszeiten?
- Ich möchte eine Stadtrundfahrt machen. Wo fährt der Bus ab?
- Wie lange dauert die Fahrt?
- Wo bekomme ich die Karten?

Jumbled dialogue
- ■ Wo fährt der Bus ab?
- □ Der Bus fährt vom Rathausmarkt ab.
- ■ Wie lange dauert die Fahrt?
- □ Drei Stunden.
- ■ Wo kann ich die Karten kaufen?
- □ Beim Fahrer.
- ■ Gibt es eine Pause?
- □ Ja, dreißig Minuten.

3 Puzzle
Bitte, Bus, Eintritt, Fahrt, Film, Platz,
rechts, Uhr

Emergencies

1 Where it happened and the name of
the hotel. 2 Fill out a form. 3 False.
4 A small and a large package. 5 Take
the medicine three times a day before
meals. 6 Yes. You should lie down.
7 An international health insurance
certificate. Yes. 8 A gas station.
9 20 liters. 10 The other driver is
going to call an ambulance.

As if you were there
At the pharmacy
- ■ Ich habe Heuschnupfen. Können
  Sie etwas empfehlen?
- ■ Ich möchte eine große Packung
  Tabletten.

At the lost and found
- ■ Ich habe meinen Mantel verloren. Ist
  mein Mantel abgegeben worden?
- ■ Er ist schwarz und aus Baumwolle.

A car breakdown
- ■ Können Sie mir helfen?
- ■ Nein, aber ich brauche Werkzeug.

At the police station
- □ Mein Name ist . . .
- □ Meine Adresse ist . . .
- □ Mein Auto wurde gestohlen.

Do you know the words?
Fundbüro, Tankstelle, internationaler
Krankenschein, Rezept, Flasche,
Packung

Dictionary

Abbiegung, die off switch
Abend, der evening
Abendessen, das evening meal
abends in the evening
aber but
abfahren to depart
Abfahrt, die departure, exit off highway
Abfahrtslauf, der downhill skiing
abgeben to hand in
Adresse, die address
Aktenkoffer, der briefcase
Alkohol, der alcohol
alkoholfrei non-alcoholic
alkoholisch alcoholic
alle everyone
Allergie, die allergy
allergisch allergic
alles everything
Altstadt, die old town
Anfang, der start, beginning
anfangen to start, to begin
angenehm pleasant
Angorawolle, die angora
Ankunft, die arrival
Anmeldeformular, das registration form
anprobieren to try on
Ansichtskarte, die postcard
anstellen to line up
Anzug, der suit (with pants)
Apfel, der apple
Apotheke, die pharmacy
Arm, der arm
Arzt, der/Ärztin, die doctor
Aschenbecher, der ashtray
auch also
auf on
Aufenthalt, der stay
Auffahrt, die entrance ramp
Aufkleber, der sticker
Aufschnitt, der cold meat
aufschreiben to write down
aufstehen to get up
Auge, das eye
aus out, from
ausfüllen to fill out
Ausgang, der exit

ausgezeichnet excellent
Auskunft, die information
aussehen to look like
außer apart from
aussteigen to get off, out
Ausstellung, die exhibition
Ausweis, der ID card, membership card
Auto, das car
Autobahn, die highway
Autonummer, die license plate number
Autowerkstatt, die garage

Bäckerei, die bakery
Bad, das bath
Badeanzug, der bathing suit
Badehose, die swimming trunks
Badekappe, die swimming hat
Badetuch, das beach towel
Badezimmer, das bathroom
Bahnhof, der train station
Bahnsteig, der platform
bald soon
Balkon, der balcony
Ball, der ball
Banane, die banana
Bank, die bank, bench
bar cash
Bar, die bar
Batterie, die battery
Bauernbrot, das bread made from sour dough
Baum, der tree
Baumwolle, die cotton
Becher, der cup, beaker
bedeuten to mean
bedienen to serve
Bedienung, die service; waiter/waitress
bei near
Beilage, die side dish
Bein, das leg
beißen to bite
bekommen to get, receive
belegtes Brot (das) sandwich
benutzen to use
Benzin, das gasoline
Berg, der hill, mountain
Bergsteigen, das mountaineering
Beruf, der job, occupation

besetat occupied, engaged, full
besser better
Besteck, das cutlery
bestellen to order
Betrieb, der, außer Betrieb out of order
Bett, das bed
bezahlen to pay
Bier, das beer
Biergarten, der beer garden
Bierkrug, der tankard
Bikini, der bikini
billig cheap
Birne, die pear, light bulb
bis until, as far as
bißchen, ein bißchen a bit of, a little of
bitte please, you're welcome
blau blue
bleiben to stay, remain
bleifrei unleaded
Bluse, die blouse
Boot, das boat
Bowle, die punch
braten to roast, bake
brauchen to need
braun brown
brechen to break
Bremse, die brake (on a vehicle)
Brezel, die pretzel
Brief, der letter
Briefmarke, die stamp
Briefpapier, das notepaper
Brieftasche, die wallet
Brille, die glasses
Brot, das bread
Brötchen, das bread roll
Brücke, die bridge
Brust, die chest
Buch, das book
buchstabieren to spell
Bügeleisen, das iron
bügeln to iron
Bus, der bus
Bushaltestelle, die bus stop
Butter, die butter

Café, das, café
Campingplatz, der campsite
CD, die CD
Cola, die cola

Creme, die cream

da there
Dame, die lady
Damenabteilung, die ladies' department
danke thank you
danken to thank
das the, that
daß that
Dia, das slide
dies this
Disko, die disco
Doppelzimmer, das double room
dort there
dort drüben over there
Dose, die can
draußen outside
dringend urgent
Drogerie, die drugstore (toiletries, not medicine)
drücken to push, press
du you (informal)
dürfen to be allowed, may
Dusche, die shower
duschen to shower

Ecke, die corner
Edamer, der Edam cheese
Ei, das, egg
Einbahnstraße, die one-way street
einfach easy; single (ticket)
Eingang, der entrance
einkaufen to buy, shop
Einkaufstasche, die shopping bag
Einkaufszentrum, das shopping center
einlösen (Geld) to exchange money
einmal once
Eintritt, der entry, admission
Eintrittskarte, die ticket (of admission)
Einzelzimmer, das single room
Eis, das ice cream
Eisdiele, die ice cream parlor
Ellbogen, der elbow
Eltern, die (pl) parents
empfehlen to recommend
Ende, das end

enthalten to contain
Entschuldigung, die excuse, apology
entwickeln to develop
er he
Erdgeschoß, das ground floor
Erkältung, die cold
Ermäßigung, die concession
erste first
Erwachsene(r), der/die adult
es it
Espresso, der espresso
essen to eat
Essen, das food
Essig, der vinegar
etwas something

fahren to drive, go
Fahrer, der driver
Fahrkarte, die ticket
Fahrplan, der schedule
Fahrrad, das bicycle
Fahrradweg, der cycle path
Fahrt, die trip, journey
Familie, die family
fangen to catch
fantastisch fantastic
Farbe, die color
Fehler, der mistake
Ferien, die (pl) holidays
Ferienappartement, das rental apartment
Fernbedienung, die remote control
Fernsehen, das television
Fernseher, der television
fertig finished, ready
Feuerwehr, die fire department
Feuerwerk, das fireworks
Feuerzeug, das (cigarette) lighter
Fieber, das fever
Film, der film, camera film
finden to find
Finger, der finger
Fisch, der fish
Fitneßraum, der gym
Flasche, die bottle
Fleisch, das meat
Fleischer, der butcher
Flunder flounder
Flughafen, der airport

Flugzeug, das airplane
Fondue, das fondue
Formular, das form
Foto, das photograph, print
Frankfurter Kranz, der Frankfurt coffee cake
Frau, die woman, Mrs.
Fräulein, das girl
frei free
Fremdenverkehrsbüro, das tourist office
freuen, es freut mich, daß I'm glad/pleased that
freuen, sich freuen auf etwas to be looking forward to something
freuen, sich freuen über etwas to be glad, pleased about something
froh happy
Frottee, das toweling
Frühstück, das breakfast
fühlen to feel
Führerschein, der driver's license
Führung, die guided tour
Fundbüro, das lost and found
funktionieren to work, function
Fuß, der foot
Fußball, der soccer
Fußballspiel, das soccer match
Fußgängerzone, die pedestrian zone
Fußknöchel, der ankle

Gabel, die fork
Galerie, die gallery
Garderobe, die cloakroom
Garten, der garden
Gaspedal, das accelerator
Gästezimmer, das guest room
Gasthaus, das guest house
Gasthof, der guest house
geben to give
geben, es gibt there is, there are
gebraten fried, roasted
gebrochen broken
Gebühr, die charge, fee
gedämpft steamed
gedünstet sautéed
gefallen, es gefällt mir I like it
gefüllt filled, stuffed
gegen against
gegenüber opposite

DICTIONARY

gegrillt grilled
Geländelauf, der cross-country run
gelb yellow
Geld, das money
gemischt mixed
Gemüse, das vegetable
Genick, das neck
Gepäck, das luggage
geradeaus straight ahead
geräuchert smoked
Gericht, das meal, dish; court
Gerstenbier, das beer made from barley
Geschäft, das business, shop
Geschäftsmann/frau, der/die business man/woman
Geschäftsreise, die business trip
Geschmack, der taste, flavor
gestern yesterday
Getränk, das drink
Glas, das glass
glauben to believe
gleich immediately
Gleis, das platform
Glück, das luck
glücklich happy
Glühbirne, die lightbulb
Golf, das golf
Golfplatz, der golf course
Golfschläger, der golf club
Goretex, das Goretex
Gramm, das gram
groß big
Größe, die size
grün green
Gurke, die cucumber
Gürtel, der belt
gut good

Haar, das hair
Haartrockner, der hair dryer
haben to have
Hafen, der harbor
halb half
Halbpension, die hotel plan that includes one meal
Hälfte, die half
hallo hello
Hals, der throat, neck
Halsschmerzen, die (pl) sore throat

halten to hold, keep
Hand, die hand
Handschuh, der glove
Handtasche, die handbag
Handtuch, das towel
Hauptbahnhof, der main station
Hauptgericht, das main course
Hauptspeise, die main course
Haus, das house
hausgemacht homemade
Haushaltsabteilung, die household goods department
heiß hot
heißen to be called
Heizung, die heating
helfen help
Hemd, das shirt
Herr, der Mr.
Herrenabteilung, die men's department
Herz, das heart
Herzanfall, der heart attack
Herzinfarkt, der heart attack
Heuriger, der young wine
Heuschnupfen der hay fever
hier here
Hilfe, die help
Hin und zurück round-trip ticket
Hinfahrkarte, die single ticket
hinter behind
hoch high
holen to get, fetch
Hörnchen, das type of croissant
Hose, die pants
Hotel, das hotel
Hüfte, die hip
Hund, der dog
husten to cough
Husten, der cough
Hustensaft, der cough medicine
Hut, der hat

ich I
Imbiß, der snack bar
in in
Infektion, die infection
Information, die information
inklusiv inclusive
Innenstadt, die city center
interessant interesting
international international

ja yes
Jacke, die jacket
Jackett, das jacket
Jägerart, die served in red wine sauce with mushrooms
Jeans, die (pl) jeans
jemand someone
Joghurt, der yogurt
Jugendherberge, die youth hostel

Kaffee, der coffee
kalt cold
Kännchen, das small pot
Karaffe, die carafe, jug
Käse, der cheese
Kasse, die till
Kassette, die cassette
Katalog, der catalogue
Kathedrale, die cathedral
Katze, die cat
kaufen to buy
Kaufhaus, das department store
Kellner/in, der/die waiter/waitress
Ketchup, der/das ketchup
Kette, die chain
Kilo, das kilo
Kilometer, der kilometer
Kind, das child
Kinderbett, das children's bed
Kinn, das chin
Kino, das cinema
Kiosk, der stand
Kirche, die church
Kirsche, die cherry
Kiwi, die kiwi fruit
Klasse, erste/zweite Klasse, die first/second class
Kleid, das dress
klein small, little
Kleingeld, das change
Klimaanlage, die air-conditioning
klingen to ring
Kneipe, die pub
Knie, das knee
Knochen, der bone
koffeinfreier Kaffee, der decaffeinated coffee
Koffer, der suitcase
kommen to come
Kommission, die commission

Kompott, das stewed fruit
Konditorei, die cake shop, café
Konferenzraum, der conference room
Konzert, das concert
Kopf, der head
Kopfschmerzen, die (pl) headache
Kopfschmerztablette, die headache tablet
Korb, der basket
kosten to cost
Kostüm, das suit (skirt and jacket)
Krankenhaus, das hospital
Krankenschein, der health insurance certificate/policy
Krankenwagen, der ambulance
Krawatte, die tie
Kreditkarte, die credit card
Kreuzung, die crossing
Kuchen, der cake
Kuckucksuhr, die cuckoo clock
Kugelschreiber, der ballpoint pen
Kuhglocke, die cow's bell
Kühler, der radiator
Kultur, die culture
kulturell cultural
Kunst, die art
Kupplung, die clutch
Kurs, der exchange rate
kurz short

lang long
langsam slow, slowly
lassen to let, leave
laufen to walk, run
Leber, die liver
Lebkuchen, der gingerbread
Leder, das leather
leid, es tut mir leid I am sorry
leider unfortunately
leihen to hire
Lenkung, die steering
Licht, das light
liegen to lie
Liegestuhl, der deck chair
Limonade, die lemonade
links left
Liter, der/das liter
Löffel, der spoon

Luft, die air
Luftpost, die airmail

machen to make, do
Magen, der stomach
Magenschmerzen, die (pl) stomachache
Mantel, der coat
Margarine, die margarine
Mark, die German deutschmark
Markt, der market
Marktplatz, der marketplace/square
Marzipantorte, die marzipan cake
Medikament, das medicine
Medizin, die medicine
Meer, das sea
mehr more
Mehrwertsteuer, die value-added tax (VAT)
Melone, die melon
Messe, die exhibition, fair
Messer, das knife
Metzger, der butcher
mieten to rent
Milch, die milk
Milchkaffee, der coffee with cream
Mineralwasser, das mineral water
mit with
Mittagessen, das lunch
mittags lunchtime
mögen to like
Mokka, der strong, black coffee
Moment, der moment
morgen tomorrow
Morgen, der morning
morgens in the morning
Moselwein, der wine from the Moselle
Motor, der engine
Mülleimer, der trash can
Mund, der mouth
Muschel, die mussel
Museum, das museum
müssen to have to, must
Mütze, die woolen hat

nach after, towards
Nachmittag, der afternoon
nachmittags in the afternoon

nächste next
Nachtisch, der dessert
Nachtklub, der nightclub
nachts at night
Nagel, der nail
nah near
Nähe, die, in der Nähe near
Name, der name
natürlich of course
neben next to
Nebenwirkung, die side effect
nehmen to take
nein no
neu new
nicht not
Nichtraucher, der non-smoker
nichts nothing
niedrig low
niemand no one
Niere, die kidney
noch yet, still
Notausgang, der emergency exit
null nought, zero
Nummer, die number
numeriert numbered
nur only
Nußtorte, die cream cake with nuts
Nylon, das nylon

oben upstairs
Ober, der waiter
Oberschenkel, der thigh
Obst, das fruit
Obstkuchen, der fruit pie
Öffnungszeit, die opening hours
oft often
ohne without
Ohr, das ear
Öl, das oil
Oper, die opera
operieren to operate
orange orange
Orangensaft, der orange juice
Ordnung, die, alles in Ordnung everything OK

Packung, die packet
Paket, das packet
Panne, die, eine Panne haben to break down, have a flat

Papier, das paper
Papiere, die (pl) ID papers
Park, der park
parken to park
Parkett, das front-row seats
Parkgebühr, die charge for parking
Parkplatz, der parking lot
passen to fit, suit, be convenient
passieren to happen, occur
Pause, die break
Penizillin, das penicillin
Pension, die boardinghouse
Person, die person
Pfeffer, der pepper
Pflaster, das adhesive bandage
Pfund, das pound
Pilsner, das Pils, strong lager
Pizza, die pizza
Plastik, das plastic
Platz im Schlafwagen, der berth
Platz, der square; place, seat
Plombe, die filling
Politik, die politics
Polizei, die police
Polizeiwache, die police station
Polizist, der policeman
Pommes frites, die (pl) french fries
Portemonnaie, das purse
Portion, die portion
Porzellan, das porcelain
Post, die post
Poster, das poster
Postkarte, die postcard
Preis, der price
pro per
probieren to taste, try
Problem, das problem
Programm, das program
Pullover, der pullover
Puppe, die doll

Quittung, die receipt

Rad, das wheel, bike
Rasierklinge, die razor blade
Rasierschaum, der shaving cream
Rastplatz, der (highway) service station
Rathaus, das town hall

rauchen to smoke
Raucher, der smoker
Rechnung, die bill
rechts right
Regen, der rain
Regenjacke, die raincoat
Regenschirm, der umbrella
regnen to rain
Reifen, der tire
Reise, die trip, journey
Reiseandenken, das souvenir
Reiseführer, der travel guide
reisen to travel
Reisepaß, der passport
Reisescheck, der traveler's check
reiten to ride
Reitunterricht, der riding lessons
Rentner/in, der/die pensioner
reservieren to reserve
Reservierung, die reservation
Restaurant, das restaurant
Rezept, das prescription
Rheinwein, der wine from the Rhine
richtig right, correct
Rock, der skirt
roh raw, underdone
Rollo, das blind
Roséwein, der rosé
rot red
Rotwein, der red wine
Rücken, der back
Rückenschmerzen, die (pl) backache
Rückfahrkarte, die round-trip ticket
Ruhe, die silence, calm, rest
ruhig quiet, still, calm

Sachertorte, die chocolate cake
Sackgasse, die cul-de-sac
Safe, der safe
Saft, der juice
sagen to say
Sahne, die cream
Salami, die salami
Salat, der salad
Salz, das salt
Sauna, die sauna
Schal, der shawl

Schale, die dessert bowl
Schalter, der counter, ticket office
schauen to look
Scheibe, die slice; window
Scheibenwischer, der windshield wiper
schicken to send
Schiff, das ship
Schinken, der ham
Schinkenwurst, die ham sausage
Schlafwagen, der sleeping car
Schläger, der racket
schlimm bad
Schloß, das castle; lock
Schlüssel, der key
schmecken to taste
Schmerz, der pain
Schmerztablette, die painkiller
Schmuck, der jewelry
Schnaps, der schnapps
Schnecke, die snail
schneiden to cut
Schokolade, die chocolate
Schokoladentorte, die chocolate cake
Scholle, die sole
schön beautiful
Schrank, der cupboard, locker
schreiben to write
Schurwolle, die pure wool
schwanger pregnant
schwarz black
Schwarzbrot, das dark bread
Schwarzwälder Schinken, der type of smoked ham
Schweinefleisch, das pork
schwierig difficult, hard
Schwimmbad, das swimming pool
schwimmen to swim
See, der lake
See, die sea
Segelboot, das sailboat
segeln to sail
Segeln, das sailing
Segelunterricht, der sailing lessons
sehen to see
sehr very
Seide, die silk
Seife, die soap

sein to be
Seite, die side
Sekt, der sparkling wine, champagne
Selbstbedienung, die self-service (in a restaurant, café)
selbsttanken self-service (gas station)
selbstverständlich of course
senden to send
Senf, der mustard
Serviette, die napkin
Shampoo, das shampoo
Show, die show
sich hinlegen to lie down
sich interessieren für to be interested in
sicher sure, certain
sie she, her, they, them
Sie you (formal)
sitzen to sit
Skiunterricht, der skiing lessons
Socke, die sock
sofort immediately
Sonne, die sun
Sonnenbrille, die sunglasses
Sonnencreme, die suntan lotion
Sonnenschirm, der umbrella
sonst noch etwas anything else
Soße, die sauce
spät late
spät, wie spät ist es? what time is it?
Speisekarte, die menu
Speisesaal, der dining room
Spezialist, der specialist
Spezialität des Hauses, die speciality of the house
Spiegel, der mirror
Spiel, das game, match
spielen to play
Sportanlage, die sports ground
Sporthalle, die sports hall
sprechen to speak, talk
Stadion, das stadium
Stadt, die town, city
Stadtplan, der map
Stadtrundfahrt, die sightseeing tour
stechen prick, sting, bite, stab
Steckdose, die plug

stehen to stand
stehlen to steal
steigen climb
stellen to put
Stellplatz, der site
Steuerrad, das steering wheel
Stiefel, der boot
Stock, der floor; story
Strand, der beach
Strandkorb, der beach chair
Straße, die street
Straßenbahn, die streetcar
Strumpf, der stocking
Strumpfhose, die tights
Stück, das piece
Stuhl, der chair
Stunde, die hour, lesson
suchen to look for
Supermarkt, der supermarket
Suppe, die soup
Surfbrett, das surfboard
surfen to surf
Surfen, das surfing
Süßigkeit, die sweet

T-Shirt, das T-shirt
Tablett, das tray
Tablette, die tablet
Tag, der day
Tagesgericht, das special
Tageskarte, die daily travel card
täglich daily
Tankstelle, die gas station
Tasche, die bag
Taschentuch, das tissue
Tasse, die cup
tauschen to exchange, change
Taxi, das taxi
Taxistand, der taxi stand
Tee, der tea
Teelöffel, der teaspoon
Teewurst, die smoked sausage spread
Telefon, das telephone
telefonieren to telephone
Telefonkarte, die telephone card
Teller, der plate
Tennis, das tennis
Tennisplatz, der tennis court
Tennisschläger, der tennis racket

Tennisspiel, das tennis match
Terrasse, die terrace
teuer expensive
Theater, das theater
Ticket, das ticket
Tisch, der table
Tischdecke, die tablecloth
Toilette, die toilet, restroom
Toilettenpapier, das toilet paper
Tomate, die tomato
Torte, die cake
Touristeninformation, die tourist information
Trainingsanzug, der sweatsuit
Traube, die grape
Traubensaft, der grape juice
Treppe, die staircase, stairs
trinken to drink
Trinkgeld, das tip
Tropfen, der drop
tschüß bye
tun to do, make

U-Bahn, die subway
Übelkeit, die sickness and nausea
über over
überfallen to attack, mug, assault
überweisen to transfer, refer
Uhr, die watch, clock
um at, around
Umkleidekabine, die locker room/cubicle
Umleitung, die detour
umsteigen to change (trains)
und and
Unfall, der accident
Unfallstation, die emergency room
ungefähr about
Universität, die university
unten downstairs
unter under
Untergeschoß, das basement
unterschreiben to sign
untersuchen to examine, investigate
Untertasse, die saucer
Untertitel, der subtitle
Urlaub, der vacation

Vegetarier, der vegetarian
vegetarisch vegetarian
Veranstaltungskalender, der entertainment guide
Verbandskasten, der first-aid kit
verbrannt burnt
Verbrennung, die burn
Verdauungsbeschwerde, die indigestion
Versicherung, die insurance
verlassen to leave, depart, check out
verletzt hurt, injured
verlieren to lose
Versicherungsnummer, die insurance number
verstehen to understand
viel much, a lot
Volleyball, der volleyball
Vollkornbrot, das whole-wheat bread
Vollpension, die hotel plan that includes three meals per day
volltanken to fill up (with gas)
von from
vor in front of, before
Vorfahrt, die right-of-way
Vorspeise, die appetizer
vorstellen to introduce
Vorstellung, die performance

wachsen to grow
wählen to choose, dial
wandern to go hiking
Wanderstock, der walking stick
wann when
warm warm
warten auf to wait for
Wartesaal, der waiting room
warum why
was what
waschen to wash
Waschsalon, der launderette
Wasser, das water
Wasserhahn, der tap
Wasserski, der water ski
Wasserski, das waterskiing
Wechselgeld, das change
wecken to wake
Wecker, der alarm clock
Weg, der path

weh tun, es tut mir weh it hurts
Wein, der wine
weiß white
Weißkohl, der cabbage
Weißwein, der white wine
weit far
weitergehen to continue
Weizenbier, das light beer, brewed with wheat
welche which
wenig little, not much
werden to become
Werkzeug, das tools
wie how
wieder again
wiedersehen, Auf Wiedersehen goodbye
willkommen, herzlich willkommen welcome
Wind, der wind
Windschutzscheibe, die windshield
windsurfen to windsurf
Windsurfen, das windsurfing
wissen to know
wo where
woher where . . . from
wohin where . . . to
wohnen to live
Wohnwagen, der camper
Wolle, die wool
Wurst, die sausage

zählen to count
zahlen to pay
Zahn, der tooth
Zahnbürste, die toothbrush
Zahnpasta, die toothpaste
Zahnschmerzen, die (pl) toothache
Zahnstocher, der toothpick
Zeh, der, toe
zeigen to show
Zeit, die time
Zeitschrift, die magazine
Zeitschriftenhändler, der newsstand
Zeitung, die newspaper
Zentrum, das center
ziehen to pull
ziemlich quite, rather, fairly

Zigarette, die cigarette
Zimmer, das room
Zimmernummer, die room
number
Zimmerschlüssel, der room key
Zitrone, die lemon
zu to, too
zuende finished, over
Zug, der train
zusammen together
Zuschlag, der supplement
Zwetschgenkuchen, der plum
cake
Zwiebelkuchen, der onion tart

Sounds German

German words are pronounced exactly the way they are written. It is actually easier than some languages, because you pronounce every letter.

Letters

Let's look at the most common consonants first, as many of them sound very similar to English:

b	**Bank**	bank
h	**Hotel**	hotel
k	**Kirche**	church
l	**links**	left
m	**Markt**	market
n	**neben**	next to
p	**Park**	park
s	**Station**	station
t	**Toilette**	toilet

Here are a few particularities about some of the consonants:

ch after **a**, **o**, **u**, **au** as in **machen** or **kuchen** sounds hard as in "kit."
Otherwise it sounds soft: **rechts**, as in the Scottish "loch," or at the end of a word as in **sechs**, it sounds like "x."

d at the end of a word as in **Bad** sounds like "t," otherwise it's pronounced like in English.

g at the end of a word as in **zwanzig** sounds like the word "ich."

j as in **ja** sounds like "y."

r as in **rot** varies in the different regions of German-speaking countries. You can either roll it with the tip of your tongue like in Spanish, or form it in the back of your throat.

s in combinations such as "st," "sp" in **Straße** or **Sport** at the beginning of a word sounds like "sht," "shp."

sch as in **Flasche** sounds like "sh."

ß as in **Straße** sounds like double "s."

v as in **vor** sounds like "f."

w as in **Wein** sounds like "v."

z as in **zehn** sounds sharp like the "ts" in "cats."